The Signature
of Jesus

THE SIGNATURE of JESUS

BRENNAN MANNING

Multnomah Books

THE SIGNATURE OF JESUS
published by Multnomah Books
A division of Random House, Inc.
© 1988, 1992, 1996 by Brennan Manning
International Standard Book Number: 1-59052-350-4

Cover image by Steve Gardner, HisImage Pixelworks

Unless otherwise indicated, Scripture quotations are from:
The Holy Bible, New International Version © 1973, 1984 by International Bible Society,
used by permission of Zondervan Publishing House.
Other Scripture quotations are from:
New American Standard Bible (NASB) © 1960, 1977, 1995 by the Lockman Foundation.
Used by permission.
The Holy Bible, King James Version (KJV).
The New Jerusalem Bible (NJB) © 1985 by Darton, Longman & Todd, Ltd. and
Doubleday & Company, Inc.
The New Testament in Modern English, Revised Edition (Phillips)
© 1958, 1960, 1972 by J. B. Phillips.
The Amplified Bible (AMP) © 1965, 1987 by Zondervan Publishing House.

Multnomah is a trademark of Multnomah Publishers
and is registered in the U.S. Patent and Trademark Office.
The colophon is a trademark of Multnomah Publishers.

Printed in the United States of America

For information:
MULTNOMAH BOOKS · 12265 ORACLE BOULEVARD, SUITE 200
COLORADO SPRINGS, CO 80921
Library of Congress Cataloging-in-Publication Data:
Manning, Brennan
The signature of Jesus: on the pages of our lives / Brennan Manning.
p. cm.
Previous ed.: Old Tappan, N.J.: Chosen Books, ©1988
ISBN 1-59052-350-4
1. Christian life—1960- 2. Jesus Christ—Person and offices. I. Title.
BV4501.2.M3376   1992
248.4—dc2092-5218
CIP

07 08 09 10—25 24 23 22

To Hillery and Ed Moise,
with gratitude
for Biloxi and Galveston,
N'awlins and Houston,
for blackened red fish and Cajun custard,
but most of all
for the signature of your love on my life.

Contents

An
OPENING
WORD

*I*N THIS BOOK I have given my heart and my language to be what it is: crude and soft-spoken, blunt and compassionate, whole and stricken, honest and provocative, drawn from the casks of life.

The prophetic word unfailingly summons the church back to the purity of the gospel and to the scandal of the Cross. In his numerous letters Paul confirms that to follow Jesus is to take the high road to Calvary. Littered along the Calvary road will lie the skeletons of our egos, the corpses of our fantasies of control, and the shards of self-righteousness, self-indulgent spirituality, and unfreedom.

The greatest need for our time is for the church to become what it has seldom been: the body of Christ with its face to the world, loving others regardless of religion or culture, pouring itself out in a life of service, offering hope to a frightened world, and presenting itself as a real alternative to the existing arrangement. "The church that is worthy of the name is a band of people in which the love of God has broken the spell of demons and false gods and which is now making a dent in the world."[1]

I want neither a blood-'n'-guts religion that would make Clint Eastwood, not Jesus, our hero; nor a speculative religion that would imprison the gospel in the halls of academia; nor a noisy, feel-good religion that is a naked appeal to emotion. I long for passion, intelligence, and compassion in a church without ostentation, gently beckoning to the world to come and enjoy the peace and unity we possess because of the Spirit in our midst.

The signature of Jesus, the Cross, is the ultimate expression of God's love for the world. The church is the church of the crucified, risen Christ only when it is stamped with his signature; only when it faces outward and moves with him along the way of the Cross. Turned inward upon itself in bickering and theological hairsplitting, the church loses its identity and its mission.

At the dawning of the twenty-first century, what separates the committed from the uncommitted is the depth and quality of our love for Jesus Christ. The superficial among us build bigger barns in the euphoria of a prosperity gospel; the trendy follow the latest fad and try to hum their way to heaven; the defeated are haunted by ghosts from the past.

But the victorious minority, unintimidated by the cultural patterns of the lockstepping majority, live and celebrate as though Jesus were near—near in time, near in place—the witness of our motives, our speech, and our behavior. As indeed he is.

Fidelity to the Word will take us along the path of *downward mobility* (Henri Nouwen's famous phrase) in the midst of an upwardly mobile world. We will find ourselves not on the path to power but on the path to powerlessness; not on the road to success but on the road to servanthood; not on the broad road of praise and popularity but on the narrow road of ridicule and rejection.

To be a Christian is to be like Christ. Somehow we must lose our life in order to find it. Christianity preaches not only a crucified God, but also crucified men and women. "May I never boast except in the cross of our Lord Jesus Christ, through which the world has been crucified to me, and I to the world" (Galatians 6:14). There is no discipleship without the Cross. I am not a follower of Jesus if I live with him only in Bethlehem and Nazareth and not in Gethsemane and on Calvary, too.

Are you called to a life of radical discipleship? To the poverty of Mother Teresa? To the prayer of the Desert Fathers? To the martyrdom of Dietrich Bonhoeffer? To the celibate lifestyle of Jesus and Paul? To a prophetic career? To full-time ministry on behalf of the downtrodden and disenfranchised? Am I?

As you think about these questions and read this book, you'll need both honesty and discernment. Not everyone is called like the rich young man to the radical renunciation of literally everything (see Mark 10:17–30).

Walter Burghardt notes:

Jesus never told Lazarus and his sisters, Martha and Mary, to give up all they had. He did not announce to Nicodemus and Joseph of Arimathea that they were excluded from the kingdom. Rich Zacchaeus proclaimed, "Look, Lord! Here and now I give half of my possessions to the poor" (Luke 19:8)—not all, just half. And still Jesus told him, "Today salvation has come to this house" (v. 9). Zacchaeus's response is good enough to inherit the kingdom. This mirrors John the Baptist replying to the crowds, "What should you do? If you have two coats, give away...one" (Luke 3:11).[2]

There are varying degrees of discipleship. Shortly after my conversion, I began secretly to envy the generosity of spirit, the profound prayer, and the spiritual gifts of others in the church community. It was an unforgettable experience of deliverance and liberation when, one day in prayer, my eyes fell on the words of the Baptist: "A man can receive only what is given him from heaven" (John 3:27).

Some of us have been so traumatized by life that simple survival, one day at a time, is our sole concern. Others have been so soiled by circumstances, scarred by physical and emotional disabilities, or bruised and battered by the vagaries of life, that they are barely able to look beyond their own needs. For example, William Barry thinks of the man from whom a legion of demons was expelled. After the cure, "as Jesus was getting into the boat, the man who had been demon-possessed begged to go with him. *Jesus did not let him*, but said, 'Go home to your family and tell them how much the Lord has done for you, and how he has had mercy on you'" (Mark 5:18–19, italics added). The man apparently did not bemoan this "rejection" as an injustice. Rather, "the man went away and began to tell in the Decapolis how much Jesus had done for him. And all the people were amazed" (v. 20).[3]

Apparently, this man was not called to radical discipleship. Yet he was called, as we are called, to listen attentively to God's first word to us. This word is the gift of ourselves to ourselves—our existence, our nature, our personal history, our uniqueness, our identity. All that we have and are is one of the unique and never-to-be-repeated ways God has chosen to express himself in space and time. Each of us, made in his image and likeness, is yet another promise he has made to the universe that he will continue to love it and care for it.

However, even when faith persuades us that we are a word of God, we may remain ignorant of what God is trying to say through us. Thomas Merton wrote, "God utters me like a word containing a partial thought of himself. A word will never be able to comprehend the voice that utters it. But if I am true to the concept that God utters in me, if I am true to the thought in him I was meant to embody, I shall be full of his actuality and find him everywhere in myself and find myself nowhere. I shall be lost in him."[4]

With endurance and perseverance we must wait for God to make clear what he wants to say through us. Such waiting involves patience and attention, as well as the courage to let yourself be spoken. This courage comes only through faith in God, *who utters no false word.*

One of the stunning lessons of the Bible is God's free use of fragile human beings to accomplish his purpose. He does not always choose the holy and devout or even the emotionally well-balanced. The venerable Liebermann, a powerful nineteenth-century missionary, was a manic-depressive who could not walk across a bridge without a compulsive desire to jump off! "The Holy Spirit is the bearer of gifts and these gifts are sometimes lavished in peculiar places."[5] God bestows his grace abundantly but unevenly. He offers no explanation why some are called to radical discipleship and others are not.

Because we all are privileged but unentitled beggars at the door of God's mercy, those called and graced to radical discipleship have no reason to boast: "But God chose the foolish things of the world to shame the wise; God chose the weak things of the world to shame the strong" (1 Corinthians 1:27).

The gift of radical discipleship is pure grace to those who have no claim to it, for the deepest desires of our heart are not in our control. Were this not so, we simply would will those desires and be done with it. The courage to live as a prophet and lover is beyond human reach. Without the grace of God, we cannot even desire God. Without the grace of God, I cannot walk the talk of Christ. All my goodwill and grim resolve could not keep me sober. In every AA meeting room in the country hangs the sign, "There, but for the grace of God, go I."

This theme is powerfully illustrated in J. D. Salinger's

novel *Franny and Zooey*. Bessie has been badgering her son Zooey to get professional help for his sister Franny. Zooey gives careful thought to the matter. Finally he says, "For a psychoanalyst to be any good with Franny at all, he'd have to be a pretty peculiar type. I don't know. He'd have to believe that it was through the grace of God that he'd been inspired to study psychoanalysis in the first place. He'd have to believe that it was through the grace of God that he wasn't run over by a…truck before he ever even got his license to practice. He'd have to believe that it's through the grace of God that he has the native intelligence to help his…patients at all. I don't know any good analysts who think along these lines. But that's the only kind of psycho-analyst who might be able to do Franny any good at all."[6]

What Jesus longs to see in radical disciples is what he saw in little children: a spirit of sheer receptivity, utter dependence, and radical reliance on the power and mercy and grace of God mediated through the Spirit of Christ. He said, "Apart from me you can do nothing" (John 15:5).

As my last book, *The Ragamuffin Gospel*, addressed the theme of radical grace, so *The Signature of Jesus* addresses radical discipleship. Discipleship is our response to grace. Whatever measure of grace we have received and to what-ever degree of discipleship we are called, every Christian stands under the Cross of Jesus Christ, wherein we find salvation.

However hidden and undramatic your witness may be, I pray that you will be daring enough to be different, humble enough to make mistakes, courageous enough to get burnt in the fire, and real enough to help others see that prose is not poetry, speech is not song, and tangibles, visibles, and perishables are not adequate for beings signed with the blood of the Lamb.

The LORD had said to Abram, "Leave your country, your people and your father's household and go to the land I will show you.

"I will make you into a great nation
and I will bless you;
I will make your name great,
and you will be a blessing.
I will bless those who bless you,
and whoever curses you I will curse;
and all peoples on earth
will be blessed through you."

So Abram left, as the LORD had told him; and Lot went with him. Abram was seventy-five years old when he set out from Haran. He took his wife Sarai, his nephew Lot, all the possessions they had accumulated and the people they had acquired in Haran, and they set out for the land of Canaan, and they arrived there.

Abram traveled through the land as far as the site of the great tree of Moreh at Shechem. At that time the Canaanites were in the land. The LORD appeared to Abram and said, "To your offspring I will give this land." So he built an altar there to the LORD, who had appeared to him.

GENESIS 12:1 — 7

Chapter One

FROM HARAN
to CANAAN

*A*s ABRAM LEAVES HARAN—"your country, your people and your father's house"—he embarks on a journey he has never made to a land he never has seen. He sets out, not because he can predict the role he is to play in the history of salvation, but simply because of his personal experience, the spiritual experience of God speaking to him. There is no program he can detail; no insight into history with which he can support his decision; no model through which he can obtain a psychological identity. Spiritual experience has become a summons: It is God who directs. And the future is God's.

God will, in time, show him the land.

God will have him father a nation.

Only God will make his life into a blessing for all the wretched and blundering children of this earth.

What is decisive at this moment for Abram is not a vision of the next twenty years, but a quality of religious experience, a present influence of God. This touches the core of faith: to believe in a personal God who calls me and leads me. Abram obeys that call. For the time being, the call is enough. Had he demanded to know more of the details and practicalities of the game plan, he would have demonstrated the antithesis of faith, for faith is never based on human assurances.

In the New Testament, Zechariah, who wanted to be sure, insisted upon some divine guarantee before yielding to God's word (see Luke 1:18). That is not faith.

The journey of the man who would become known as Abraham is a paradigm of all authentic faith. His is a movement into obscurity, into the undefined, into ambiguity, and not into some predetermined, clearly delineated plan for the future. Each future determination, each next step discloses itself only out of a discernment of the influence of God in the present moment. "By faith Abraham, when called to go to a place he would later receive as his inheritance, obeyed and went, *even though he did not know where he was going*" (Hebrews 11:8, italics mine). The reality of life for Christian men and women requires that they leave what is nailed down, obvious, and secure, and walk into the desert without rational explanations to justify their decisions or guarantee their future. Why? Solely and simply because God signals this movement and offers it his promise.

It is instructive to remember that prior to his encounter with the one true God, Abraham, like everyone else in his tribe and country of Haran, had held many religious beliefs. (Even an atheist has them, for not to believe in God is, in itself, a religious belief.[1]) What happened to Abraham was that he was summoned by God from these religious beliefs to faith—an enormous step.

For contemporary Christians, there is an essential difference between belief and faith. Our religious beliefs are the visible expression of our faith, our personal commitment to the person of Jesus. However, if the Christian beliefs inherited from our family and passed on to us by our church tradition are not grounded in a shattering, life-changing experience of Jesus as the Christ, then the chasm between our creedal statements and our faith-experience widens and our witness is worthless. The gospel will persuade no one unless it has so convicted us that we are transformed by it.

After two thousand years of church history, why is our world's population less than one-third Christian? Why are the personalities of many pious Christians so opaque? Why did Friedrich Nietzsche reproach Christians for "not looking like they are saved"? Why do we so seldom hear in our day what the old lawyer said of John Vianney, "An extraordinary thing happened to me today: I saw Christ in a man"? Why don't our contagious joy, enthusiasm, and gratitude infect others with a longing for Christ? Why are the fire and spirit of Peter and Paul so conspicuously absent from our pallid existence?

Perhaps because so few of us have undertaken the journey of faith across the chasm between knowledge and experience. We prefer to read the map rather than visit the place. The specter of our actual unbelief persuades us that it is not the experience that is real but, rather, our explanation of the experience. Our beliefs—which William Blake called "the mind-forged manacle"—distance us from the grip of personal experience.

Daniel Taylor writes:

> The secular world of ideas plays the doubting game almost exclusively and is usually scornful of anyone who doesn't. Ironically, however, the church also plays this game to a great extent. The mystery of the gospel, the paradox of the incarnation, and the wondrous enigma of grace are freeze-dried into a highly rationalized and/or authoritarian system of theologies, codes, rules, prescriptions, orders of service, and forms of church government. Everything is written down, everything is organized, so that all can be certain and those in error detected.[2]

The movement from Haran to Canaan is the journey across the chasm. We have to pass definitively beyond beliefs to faith. Yes, we are called to believe in Jesus. But our belief summons us to something greater, to *faith* in him. Faith that will force us to pursue the mind of Christ, to embrace a lifestyle of prayer, unselfishness, goodness, and involvement in building his kingdom, not our own.

When God called Abraham to abandon the security of the world familiar to him, he also asked Abraham to forsake his polytheistic religious beliefs. All his previous concepts of God faded away. The same process is necessary for us. When we encounter the God revealed by and in Jesus Christ, we must revise all our previous thinking about God. Jesus, as the revealer of the Godhead, defines God as love. In light of this revelation, we have to abandon the cankerous, worm-eaten structure of legalism, moralism, and perfectionism that corrupts the Good News into an ethical code rather than a love affair.

Jesus lanced the infection of religious belief that had lost its soul and did not even know it. The Pharisees had distorted the image of God into some remote bookkeeper who is constantly snooping around after sinners (and one day will nail us if our accounts are not in order). The Pharisees were so busy refining and finessing the formulas of religion, so assiduous in studying what they believed, that they forgot the reality their beliefs signified. They had believed for so long but their faith had dulled. They had awaited the Messiah for so long, their expectancy was blunted.

And yet, despite Jesus' condemnation of pharisaic religion, the spirit of legalism, "like the vilest seed of the overgrown Garden, has flourished on the trellis of the centuries."[3] Many Christians remain afraid, for they still cling to an idea of God very different from that preached by Jesus. They remain in Haran with their old belief system intact. They believe they can save themselves by holding still and not breathing or by embarking on fasts, vigils, or heroic enterprises, hoping to coax approbation from God.

Again and again Jesus stated that fear is the enemy of life.

"Don't be afraid; just believe" (Luke 8:50).

"Do not be afraid, little flock, for your Father has been pleased to give you the kingdom" (Luke 12:32).

"Take courage! It is I. Don't be afraid" (Matthew 14:27).

Fear breeds a deadening caution, a holding back, a stagnant waiting until people no longer can recall what they are waiting for or saving themselves for. When we fear failure more than we love life; when we are dominated by thoughts of what we might have been rather than by thoughts of what we might become; when we are haunted by the disparity between our ideal self and our real self; when we are tormented by guilt, shame, remorse, and self-condemnation, we deny our faith in the God of love. God calls us to break camp, abandon the comfort and security of the status quo, and embark in perilous freedom on the journey to a new Canaan. But when we procrastinate out of fear, this represents not only a decision to remain in Haran, but also a lack of trust.

My own faltering faith caused me to procrastinate regarding God's call to marry Roslyn. I postponed the decision for three years (which was a decision itself) hoping that God would grow weary of waiting and the inner voice of Truth would get laryngitis. Before leaving the familiar landscape of the Franciscan life, I wanted God to sketch out definite lines so that I might know explicitly where I was going. Of course, authentic faith eludes such certainty. It means we cannot cling to anything. We always must leave something behind and not look back (see Luke 9:62). If we refuse to keep moving and insist on signs and tangible proofs, we diminish our faith, and that means unbelief. Ironically, throughout the entire process my religious beliefs remained steadfast and unwavering.

The God of Abraham, who is the God and Father of Jesus Christ, is not a threat. The certainty that he wants us to live, to grow, to unfold, and to experience fullness of life is the basic premise of authentic faith. Yet my reluctance to pray the prayer of abandonment of Charles de Foucauld— "Father, do with me whatever you want"—reveals that I am still in the iron grip of skepticism and fear: *Letting God have at me may jeopardize my health, my reputation, and my security. He might strip me of my red suspenders and Rolex and send me off to Tanzania as a missionary. If he would just let me stay in the temple of my familiar, I would entrust myself to him wholeheartedly.*

Biblical faith is an attitude acquired gradually through many crises and trials. Through the agonizing test with his son Isaac (see Genesis 22:1–19), Abraham learns that God wants us to live and not to die, to grow and not to wither. He knows that the God who called him to hope against hope is reliable. "Perhaps this is the essence of faith: to be convinced of the reliability of God."[4]

Louis Evely tells the story of an old woman who read Renan's *Vie de Jesus* and many other "breviaries of skepticism." She declared, "I simply can't believe that Christ is God. If he were, he'd have given me some proof, for I've wanted so sincerely to believe in him." She had not wanted to believe at all; she wanted to *know,* to discover some fact that would satisfy her intellect. But real faith does not reside in the intellect alone. The Truth who is Christ is not something purely rational. When we love

eone, a thousand arguments do not make one proof,
do a thousand objections make one doubt.[5]

If there is one thing I have learned in the gathering mist
of midlife, it is that the journey from Haran to Canaan is a
personal one. Each of us bears the responsibility of responding to the call of Christ individually and committing ourselves to him personally. Do I believe in Jesus or in the
preachers, teachers, and cloud of witnesses who have spoken
to me *about* him? Is the Christ of my belief really my own or
that of theologians, pastors, parents, and Oswald
Chambers? No one—parents, friends, or church—can
absolve us of this ultimate personal decision regarding the
nature and identity of the son of Mary and Joseph. His
question to Peter, *Who do you say that I am?* is addressed to
every would-be disciple.

Let us take some time to reflect on the credibility of the
One who calls us. He asks me to risk everything on his
claim that he is the way, the truth, and the life. Unlike
Buddha, Muhammad, and other founders of great world
religions, he invites me not simply to believe in his teaching, but to place all my faith in him. Who is this Nazarene
carpenter who dares to demand surrender to himself?

His family tree is less than impressive. In Matthew's
genealogy of Jesus, the son of David, the son of Abraham,
Matthew includes the names of a few women with shady
reputations: Tamar, the daughter-in-law of Judah, disguises
herself as a prostitute in order to get pregnant by him (see
Genesis 38:12–30); Rahab is the famous prostitute of
Jericho (see Joshua 2:1); and Bathsheba, who gave birth to
a child following an adulterous act with King David who,

when he failed to disguise his own paternity, murdered her husband, Uriah (see 2 Samuel 11).

Obviously, God does not necessarily elect those of unimpeachable pedigree to do his work in this world.[6] In their book *Toxic Faith*, Steve Arterburn and Jack Felton list twenty-one toxic beliefs of toxic faith. "God uses only spiritual giants" is prominent on the list:

> Many fail to receive the blessings that come from ministering to others because of the belief that God uses only the perfect or the near perfect.... In my life as well as in Scripture, I have seen nothing but the opposite to be true. God often uses those who have major flaws or who have been through a great deal of pain to accomplish many vital tasks for his kingdom.... No one is too messed up for God to use.[7]

Yes, the genealogy of Jesus does not inspire messianic confidence. What of his birth? Obscure? Yes, absolutely, unimpressively obscure. The circumstances of his conception are jarring, to put it mildly. ("Well, just imagine yourself trying to tell someone that your son, whom they know to have been born seven months after your wedding, and whom they consider with good cause to be a threat to both civil and ecclesiastical law and order, was conceived by the Holy Spirit!"[8])

Thirty years later this relatively uneducated Galilean peasant goes to the Jordan River to be baptized by John's baptism of repentance for the forgiveness of sins. His career is launched. He becomes neither statesman nor economist, neither general nor renowned author, though he was certainly a storyteller and something of a poet. As he roamed about the countryside, his family decided he needed custodial care (see Mark 3:21). The religious leaders of his day suspected a demonic seizure (see Mark 3:22), and bystanders called him some very bad names. Eventually he was executed as a heretic, blasphemer, false prophet, and seducer of the people after due legal trial before the highest courts of the land.

This is God's Son? This is the man who calls me to dedicate my entire life to him? Who tells me life has no meaning apart from him?

That the source of our faith could be found in a man whose birth was obscure and therefore vulnerable to suspicion and who died the death of a criminal; that the substance of our faith should consist in the conviction that illegitimates, sinners, and criminals can say "Abba" to God; that hookers can enter into God's kingdom before the religiously respectable—that is not a vision of faith accessible to speculation or common sense!

Simply reading the Bible cannot of itself yield the Christian faith commitment. Neither the beliefs of my parents, teachers, or church, nor the witness of friends, neither cult nor creed, neither code nor institution, neither books such as this one nor a thousand sermons by Billy Graham, Tony Campolo, and Chuck Swindoll can, of themselves, yield the Christian faith commitment.

The possibility of anyone's recognizing in the fragile humanity of Jesus the plentitude of God's power to save comes only from a miraculous intervention of God. "Radical faith is not an achievement, for if it were we would will it and be done. Rather, it is a gift, and we are left to react respectively, to watch and to pray."[9] Paul, writing to the Corinthians, recognizes that the Spirit, handed over by Jesus, makes possible the most basic act of the Christian life: "No one can say, 'Jesus is Lord,' except by the Holy Spirit" (1 Corinthians 12:3).

The faith that Jesus inspired in his disciples had such a profound impact on them that the disciples found it impossible to believe anyone could be equal to him or greater, not even Moses or Elijah, not even Abraham. That a prophet or judge or Messiah should come after Jesus and be greater than Jesus was inconceivable. It was not necessary to wait for someone else. Jesus was everything. Jesus was everything the Jews had ever hoped and prayed for. Jesus had fulfilled, or was about to fulfill, every promise and every prophecy. If anyone is to judge the world in the end, it must be he. If anyone is to be appointed Messiah, King, Lord, Son of God, how could it be anyone but Jesus?

"Jesus was experienced as *the* breakthrough in the history of humankind. He transcended everything that ever had been said and come before. He was in every way the ultimate, the last word. He was on a par with God. His word was God's word. His Spirit was God's Spirit. His feelings were God's feelings. What he stood for was exactly the same as what God stood for. No higher estimation was possible."[10]

This was the experience of Jesus' followers. Contemporary Christian faith resonates with the evaluation of the primitive church. In a real sense, Jesus is our faith. As I wrote elsewhere, "We are not travel agents handing out brochures to places we have never visited." We are faith-explorers of a country without borders, one we discover, little by little, not to be a place but a person. Our faith includes our beliefs, but it also transcends them, for the reality of Jesus Christ never can be confined within doctrinal formulations.

The question henceforth is no longer *Is Jesus God-like?* but *Is God Jesus-like?* This is the traditional meaning of the assertion that Jesus is the Word of God. "Jesus reveals God to us, God does not reveal Jesus to us."[II] We cannot deduce anything about Jesus from what we think we know about God; we must now deduce everything about God from what we do know about Jesus.

Like Abraham, all our previous images of God fade away.

The gift of my own faith in Jesus Christ does not depend or rely upon any power outside of my experience of God's grace. When beliefs replace actual experience; when we no longer *know* but come to rely on the authority of books, institutions, or leaders; when we let religion interpose between us and the primary experience of Jesus as the Christ, we lose the reality religion itself describes as ultimate.

Incidentally, herein lies the origin of all holy wars as well as the bigotry, intolerance, and division within the body of Christ. Nothing ever has failed for Christianity as much as the Crusades. One grows dizzy counting the battles allegedly fought about the nature of "true" faith. Clashes of beliefs lie beneath the terrorism that makes the headlines every day, "and the intimidation that is exercised more anonymously but just as righteously to urge ordinary people into practices and sects that claim to have the secret combination to God's treasure-house of favor."[12]

After twenty-two years of living by secondhand faith, on February 8, 1956, I met Jesus and moved from Haran to Canaan—from belief to faith. It was noon. The Angelus bell from the cloistered Carmelite monastery sounded in the distance. I was kneeling in a small chapel in Loretto, Pennsylvania. At five minutes after three, I rose shakily from the floor, knowing that the greatest adventure of my life had just begun. I entered a new perspective accurately described by Paul in Colossians 3:11: "Christ is all, and is in all."

> During those three hours on my knees, I felt like a little boy kneeling at the seashore. Little waves washed up and lapped against my knees. Slowly the waves grew bigger and stronger until they reached my waist. Suddenly a tremendous wave of concussion force knocked me over backward and swept me off the beach, reeling in midair, arching through space, vaguely aware that I was being carried to a place I had never been before—the heart of Jesus Christ....
>
> In this first-ever-in-my-life experience of being unconditionally loved, I moved back and

forth between ecstasy and fear.... The moment lingered on and on in a timeless *now* until, without warning, a hand gripped my heart. I could barely breathe. The awareness of being loved was no longer gentle, tender, and comfortable. The love of Christ, the crucified Son of God, took on the wildness, fury, and passion of a sudden spring storm. *Jesus died on the cross for me!*

I had known that before, but in the way that John Henry Newman describes as "notional knowledge"—abstract, faraway, largely irrelevant to the gut issues of life, just another trinket in the dusty pawnshop of doctrinal beliefs. But in one blinding moment of salvific truth it was *real* knowledge calling for personal engagement of my mind and heart. Christianity was being loved and falling in love with Jesus Christ. Later the words in the first letter of Peter would illuminate and verify my experience: "You did not see him, yet you love him; and still without seeing him, you are already filled with a joy so glorious that it cannot be described, because you believe; and you are sure of the end to which your faith looks forward, that is, the salvation of your soul" (1:8−9).

At last, drained, spent, feeling limp and lost in speechless humility, I was back kneeling at the seashore with quiet, calm waves of love sweeping over me like a gentle tide saturating my mind and heart in a tranquil mode of deep worship.[13]

On that day I knew God's love and power—the essence of Christian faith. We must know God's love and power with a knowledge greater than our knowledge because it is beyond the capacity of mere human knowledge. We must know this with the mind of Christ himself. This is the basic redemptive Christian encounter. This is the movement from belief to experience via the bridge of faith.

In order to commit ourselves to radical discipleship, in order to live with the signature of Jesus written on the pages of our lives, we need the strength and encouragement of other Christians. But our deepest need is for the inexhaustible power of the love of Christ. The miracle of Christianity is that this need is already met. Through a serious life of prayer we become aware that we already have what we seek. In faith we come into consciousness of what is already there (more on this later). The power dwells within us, so far exceeding our need that conscious contact with it sweeps us out of ourselves beyond anything we could have imagined or desired and into the reality that is Christ.

Recently, I was given a copy of a note found written in the office of a young pastor in Zimbabwe, Africa, following his martyrdom for his faith in Jesus Christ. I quote his letter verbatim:

I'm part of the fellowship of the unashamed. I have the Holy Spirit's power. The die has been cast. I have stepped over the line. The decision has been made—I'm a disciple of his. I won't look back, let up, slow down, back away, or be still. My past is redeemed, my present makes sense, my future is secure. I'm finished and done with low living, sight walking, smooth knees, colorless dreams, tamed visions, worldly talking, cheap giving, and dwarfed goals.

I no longer need preeminence, prosperity, position, promotions, plaudits, or popularity. I don't have to be right, first, tops, recognized, praised, regarded, or rewarded. I now live by faith, lean in his presence, walk by patience, am uplifted by prayer, and I labor with power.

My face is set, my gait is fast, my goal is heaven, my road is narrow, my way rough, my companions are few, my Guide reliable, my mission clear. I cannot be bought, compromised, detoured, lured away, turned back, deluded, or delayed. I will not flinch in the face of sacrifice, hesitate in the presence of the enemy, pander at the pool of popularity, or meander in the maze of mediocrity.

I won't give up, shut up, let up, until I have stayed up, stored up, prayed up, paid up, preached up for the cause of Christ. I am a disciple of Jesus. I must go till he comes, give till I drop, preach till all know, and work till he stops me. And, when he comes for his own, he will have no problem recognizing me...my banner will be clear!

Perhaps the only honest measure of authentic faith is my readiness for martyrdom. Not only my willingness to die for Jesus Christ and the sake of the gospel, but to live for him one day at a time.

The Cross is the permanent signature of the risen Christ. The signed lifestyle requires a faith devoid of sentiment, ecstasies, and vision. "We live by faith, not by sight" (2 Corinthians 5:7). While faith is a gift of God, it calls for rugged effort on our part if it is to bear fruit. Modern-day hermit Carlo Caretto writes, "God gives us the boat and the oars, but then tells us, 'It's up to you to row.' Making positive acts of faith is like training this faculty; it is developed by training as the muscles are developed by gymnastics."

This book is not a mincing pastoral, nor a series of well-behaved meditations for pious people. It is a book about being heroes and heroines for the sake of Jesus Christ—for the sake of no one less than Christ, and in such a fashion that only the eyes of Jesus need see. It is a summons to authentic faith and radical discipleship, to the purity of the gospel, to the high road to Calvary and the scandal of the Cross, to a life of freedom under the signature of Jesus.

In the last analysis, faith is not the sum of our beliefs or a way of speaking or a way of thinking; it is a way of living and can be articulated adequately only in a living practice. To acknowledge Jesus as Savior and Lord is meaningful insofar as we try to live as he lived and to order our lives according to his values. We do not need to theorize about Jesus; we need to make him present in our time, our culture, and our circumstances. Only a true practice of our Christian faith can verify what we believe. As the French philosopher Maurice Blondel was fond of saying, "If you really want to understand what a man believes, don't listen to what he says, but watch what he does."

A simple suggestion: Each time you turn a page of this book, whisper the words, "Lord, increase my faith."

Chapter Two

THE SIGNATURE
of JESUS

I KNOW A MAN who for twenty-five years has refused to allow a cross or a crucifix in his home. Far from being superficial, he is a person of integrity. He doesn't shout with the crowd, nor does he dismiss Christianity as a musty antique of a medieval past. Why then does he refuse? In his own words, "I can't stand the Cross. It is a denial of all that I value in life. I am a proud man, sensual, I seek pleasure. The Cross reproaches me. It says, 'You're wrong. Your life must take this shape. This is the only true interpretation of life, and life is true only when it takes this form.'" And so, he will not allow a symbol of the cru- cified Christ in his home. In his honesty he knows that to do so, he must commit himself to a way of life that contradicts the life he is living.

This story of one man's flight from God is nothing new. Francis Thompson told it more than a hundred years ago in poetry when he wrote:

> Down the nights and down the days...
> I fled Him, down the labyrinthine ways
> of my own mind; and in the mist of tears
> I hid from Him, and under running laughter.

And the Hound of Heaven replies:

> "Lo, all things fly thee, for thou fliest Me!
> Strange, piteous, futile thing."[1]

For the apostle Paul, hostility to the Cross is the foremost characteristic of the world. To the Galatians Paul writes that what stamps Christians most deeply is the fact that through Jesus' cross the world is crucified to him and he to the world. To the Corinthians, Paul says we manifest the life of Jesus only if we carry his death about with us. What Paul says to them applies to every Christian. We are disciples only as long as we stand in the shadow of the Cross.

The Master said that he who "does not take his cross and follow me is not worthy of me" (Matthew 10:38). Dietrich Bonhoeffer, the German martyr, caught the meaning of this when he wrote, "When Jesus calls a man, he bids him come and die."[2] We have no reason or right to choose another way than the way God chose in Jesus Christ. The Cross is both the symbol of our salvation and the pattern of our lives.

When our dogmatic beliefs and moral principles do not realize themselves in discipleship, then our holiness is an illusion. And the world has no time for illusions. Today the Christian community does not disturb the world. Why should it? The cross is as commonplace on a pierced earring of the rock singer Madonna as it is on a tombstone.

Christian piety has trivialized the passionate God of Golgotha. Christian art has turned the unspeakable outrage of Calvary into dignified jewelry. Christian worship has sentimentalized monstrous scandal into sacred pageant. Organized religion has domesticated the crucified Lord of glory, turned him into a tame symbol. Viewed as a church relic, the cross does not disturb our comfortable religiosity. But when the crucified, risen Christ, instead of remaining an icon, comes to life and delivers us over to the fire he came to light, he creates more havoc than all the heretics, secular humanists, and self-serving preachers put together.

There is a frightening preoccupation with trivia in the American church today. With the gravity of a hanging judge, we quibble over the songs we sing and the songs we refuse to sing. William Penn said, "To be like Christ is to be a Christian."[3] And Jesus demands nothing less than the placing of our own egos and desires on the Cross. Today many churches attempt to eliminate the risk and danger of this call. We cushion the risk and remove the danger of discipleship by drawing up a list of moral rules that give us security instead of holy insecurity. The Word of the Cross, the power and wisdom of Jesus Christ crucified, is conspicuous by its absence.

Recently a friend called me long distance to ask if I was upset by what a certain television evangelist said on his program about Roman Catholics. I replied that nothing he says upsets me; it's what he doesn't say that upsets me. Dr. Martin Marty, Lutheran professor of church history at the University of Chicago, puts it this way: "The problem is that Christianity and celebrity don't go together. A celebrity has a big ego and needs to feed it. These shows misportray government, humanism, and mainline religions. They don't convert; they confirm. I can't picture them changing people."

But changing people is the point—weaning us from our worldly values. The apostle Paul was aware of the worldliness that had penetrated and gained ground within the church. He said there were enemies of the Cross of Christ in Galatia and Corinth, in Philippi and Rome—not so much among the waverers as among the most devout church members. Jesus did not die at the hands of muggers, rapists, or thugs. He fell into the well-scrubbed hands of priests and lawyers, statesmen and professors—society's most respected members.

In his book *The Cost of Discipleship*, Bonhoeffer defined "cheap grace" as grace without the Cross.[4] When Jesus Christ crucified is not proclaimed and lived out in love, the church is a bored and boring society. There is no power, no challenge, no fire. No change. We make drab what ought to be dramatic. A Christian is a lover of Christ and his Cross.

Returning to Ernst Kasemann:

> A man counts as a lover of the cross only insofar as
> it enables him to come to terms with himself and
> others and with the powers and enticements of
> the world. Under the cross, man attains man-
> hood…there is no sharing in the glory of the risen
> Lord except in the discipleship of the cross.[5]

In April 1944, a year before his death, while impris-
oned in a concentration camp in Flossenburg, Germany,
Bonhoeffer wrote, "What is bothering me incessantly is
the question of what Christianity really is, or indeed what
Christ really is for us today."[6] That is the question each of
us must spell out for himself. Who is Jesus? What does
discipleship today involve? Everything else is a distraction.

The Jesus of my journey is the crucified one. The sign
of his lordship is the Cross and the Cross alone. It is the
signature of the risen one. The glorified Christ is identifi-
able with the historical Jesus of Nazareth only as the Man
of the Cross.

So central to the story of salvation is the signature of
Jesus that Paul does not hesitate to say, "For I resolved to
know nothing…except Jesus Christ and him crucified"
(1 Corinthians 2:2). When Paul arrived in Corinth, he
had just returned from Athens, where he had become
discouraged by his failure to win the Greek community
through his use of natural theology. To the people of this
licentious seaport town of Corinth where sexual

immorality flourished, Paul abandoned the wisdom approach and preached instead the folly of the Cross.

In a stunning paradox, Paul tells the Corinthians:

> For the message of the cross is foolishness to those who are perishing, but to us who are being saved it is the power of God. Jews demand miraculous signs and Greeks look for wisdom, but we preach Christ crucified: a stumbling block to Jews and foolishness to Gentiles, but to those whom God has called, both Jews and Greeks, Christ the power of God and the wisdom of God. For the foolishness of God is wiser than man's wisdom, and the weakness of God is stronger than man's strength. (1 Corinthians 1:18, 22–25)

The Greek word for "foolishness" suggests something that is dull, insipid—stupid not in the sense of being publicly dangerous, but publicly despised, ignored because it is ridiculous. And this is precisely what Paul proclaims. His revelation runs directly counter to the expectations of Jew and Greek. The Jews looked for a Messiah, but Jesus' shameful death on a cross proved to them that he wasn't the glorious liberator they awaited. The Cross formed an obstacle to faith.

The Greeks were sure that the Messiah would be a philosopher greater than Plato, able to demonstrate the order and harmony of the universe. A Messiah who would challenge this cultured, intellectual piety by reversing its values and dying on a cross, a victim of the irrational and bestial in humankind, would indeed be a stupidity to the Greeks.

Yet Paul preached the Word of the Cross in the power of the Spirit, and experienced astonishing success. Jews and Greeks alike laid aside their prejudices to be swept up by the power and wisdom of the Cross. For the Cross is not a message about suffering but the suffering Christ "who loved me and gave Himself up for me" (Galatians 2:20, NASB).

Good Friday reminds us that we are not going to be helped by power, only by God's laying aside his power for love of us. Power forces us to change; only love can move us to change. Power affects behavior; love affects the heart. And nothing on earth so moves the heart as suffering love. That is why the perfect expression of God's love for us is the dying figure of Jesus pleading for someone to moisten his burning lips.

In the winter of 1968, I lived in a cave in the mountains of the Zaragosa Desert in Spain. For seven months I saw no one, never heard the sound of a human voice. Hewn out of the face of the mountain, the cave towered six thousand feet above sea level. Each Sunday morning a brother from the village of Farlete below dropped off food, drinking water, and kerosene at a designated spot. Within the cave a stone partition divided the chapel on the right from the living quarters on the left. A stone slab covered with potato sacks served as a bed. The other furniture was a rugged granite desk, a wooden chair, a Sterno stove, and a kerosene lamp. On the wall of the chapel hung a three-foot crucifix. I awoke each morning at 2:00 and went into the chapel for an hour of nocturnal adoration.

On the night of December 13, during what began as a long and lonely hour of prayer, I heard in faith Jesus Christ say, "For love of you I left my Father's side. I came to you who ran from me, fled me, who did not want to hear my name. For love of you I was covered with spit, punched, beaten, and affixed to the wood of the cross."

These words are burned on my life. Whether I am in a state of grace or disgrace, elation or depression, that night of fire quietly burns on. I looked at the crucifix for a long time, figuratively saw the blood streaming from every pore of his body, and heard the cry of his wounds: "This isn't a joke. It is not a laughing matter to me that I have loved you." The longer I looked, the more I realized that no man has ever loved me and no one ever could love me as he did. I went out of the cave, stood on the precipice, and shouted into the darkness, "Jesus, are you crazy? Are you out of your mind to have loved me so much?"

I learned that night what a wise old man had told me years earlier: "Only the one who has experienced it can know what the love of Jesus Christ is. Once you have experienced it, nothing else in the world will seem more beautiful or desirable."

The Lord reveals himself to each of us in myriad ways. For me the human face of God is the strangulating Jesus stretched against a darkening sky. In another of his letters from prison, Bonhoeffer wrote, "This is the only God who counts." Christ on the cross is not a mere theological precondition for salvation. He is God's enduring Word to the world saying, "See how much I love you. See how you must love one another."

Christian love is, in essence, neither romantic nor heroic, writes theologian John Shea, but in a world that calls Christians who are trying to live the Sermon on the Mount naive, irrelevant, unrealistic, simplistic, and even mad, the disciple of Jesus simply tries "to stand fast a little," vulnerable to taunts and lances.

A Polish Jew who survived the massacre of the Warsaw ghetto, and later converted to Christianity, discovered that on the acceptance or rejection of the Crucified hangs the meaning of discipleship: "As I looked at that man upon the Cross…I knew I must make up my mind once and for all, and either take my stand beside Him and share in His undefeated faith in God…or else fall finally into a bottomless pit of bitterness, hatred, and unutterable despair."[7]

The Christ of the New Testament is not the God of the philosophers, speaking with detachment about the Supreme Being. We do not expect to find the Supreme Being with spit on his face. It jars us to discover that the invitation Jesus issues is, *Don't weep for me; join me. The life I have planned for you is a Christian life, much like the life I led.*

As Dominique Voillaume once said to me on a wintry morning in Dijon, France, "*La vie est dure.*" Life is hard. It is hard to be a Christian, but it is too dull to be anything else. When Jesus comes into our lives with his scandalous Cross in the form of mental anguish, physical suffering, and wounds of the spirit that will not close, we pray for the courage to "stand fast a little" against the insidious realism of the world, the flesh, and the devil.

The signature of Jesus: the Cross. For me the most difficult and demanding dimension of discipleship on a day-in, day-out basis is the commitment to a life of unending avail-ability. In the early stage of my journey, in the first flush of full love, the imitation of the Ebed Yahweh, God the Servant, was a romantic, even intoxicating notion. Tonight on this warm Louisiana evening, being a servant is as unsen-timental as duty, as steadily demanding as need. Hurting people are always there, and sometimes the power of their need, like a suction on my spirit, drains me of everything. One of my problems with Jesus is that he always seems to come at the wrong time. Small wonder that Teresa of Avila complained, "Lord, if this is the way you treat your friends, it's no surprise you have so few."

In words to this effect, Jesus told his listeners, "A sign indeed you will have, but it will not be the sign of the Romans being driven into the sea, or of the sun growing dark; it will be a sign of the Servant of Yahweh to be mani-fested first in my life and then in my death, and after that in the lives of my disciples. Their joyous commitment to the Good News of my Father's kingdom will issue in lives of service that will permit no doubt about the validity of my message. The ultimate credentials I offer as spokesman for my heavenly father will be the kind of lives I and my followers after me will live."

A beautiful game plan. If indeed we lived a life in imi-tation of his, our witness would be irresistible. If we dared to live beyond our self-concern; if we refused to shrink from being vulnerable; if we took nothing but a compas-sionate attitude toward the world; if we were a countercul-ture to our nation's lunatic lust for pride of place, power, and possessions; if we preferred to be faithful rather than successful, the walls of indifference to Jesus Christ would crumble. A handful of us could be ignored by society; but hundreds, thousands, millions of such servants would over-whelm the world. Christians filled with the authenticity, commitment, and generosity of Jesus would be the most spectacular sign in the history of the human race. The call of Jesus is revolutionary. If we implemented it, we would change the world in a few months.

Several years ago *Reader's Digest* featured these five articles: "How to Stay Slim Forever," "Five Ways to Stop Feeling Tired," "How to Get Your Way," "How Safe Are the New Contraceptives?" and "What It Takes to Be Successful." The editors apparently concluded that the majority of Americans are fat, exhausted, frustrated, lasciv-ious, and dissatisfied with their level of achievement. The editors may be right; if so, there is a breathtaking superfi-ciality to our alleged interests.

The conversation of most middle-class Americans, we are told, revolves around consumption: what to buy, what was just bought, where to eat, what to eat, the price of the neighbor's house, what's on sale this week, our clothes or someone else's, the best car on the market this year, where to spend a vacation. Apparently we can't stop eating, shop-ping, or consuming. Success is measured not in terms of love, wisdom, and maturity but by the size of one's pile of possessions.[8]

What was it Ernst Kasemann said? "A man counts as a lover of the cross only insofar as it enables him to come to terms with...the powers and enticements of the world." What is outrageous about the disciple of Jesus is that he can afford to be indifferent. Dead to the world but gloriously alive in Christ, he can say with Paul, "I know how to be stuffed full, and I know how to be destitute." Such an attitude is anathema to Madison Avenue. The world will respect us if we court it, and it will respect us even more if we reject it in disdain or anger; but it will hate us if we simply take no notice of its priorities or what it thinks of us. There is a radical incompatibility between human respect and faith in Jesus Christ.

It is 1:30 A.M. I go to my darkened study, turn on the overhead spotlight that shines on the crucifix, and stare at the body naked and nailed. Prostrate on the floor, I whisper, "Come, Lord Jesus" over and over. I pray with the powerlessness and poverty of a child, knowing that I cannot free myself—I must be set free. Simply showing up at the appointed time, allowing God to make the changes in me that I cannot make myself.

What can happen in prayer is described in a scene in *Man of La Mancha*.

In the play a dialogue takes place between Alonso Chiana (aka Don Quixote) and Aldonza, a barmaid and hooker. In his delusion, Alonso sees this tramp as an aristocrat and treats her accordingly. He calls this coarse, vulgar trollop "my lady" and "Dulcinea, my sweet little one." At first she is puzzled and angry. She can't understand this madman. But there is a haunting beauty about him. Why is she attracted to this mysterious man? Because out of him comes an affirmation that she is treasure and is to be prized as treasure and treated as treasure. He shatters her wall of defensiveness and fear.

"Dulcinea!" cries Aldonza. "My God, he knows my whole life story. I'm a slut. Yet he is calling me Dulcinea!" For this woman covered with shame, it is a word that rises like a beacon from the depths of a black sea. Dazzling in its simplicity, transforming in its power, astounding in its wisdom, *Dulcinea* is unspeakable utterance from the mystical depths of God himself. *Dulcinea* is stunning revelation that God reads everything differently from the way we do. You cannot miss what he is up to in his servant Don Quixote: The losers will be winners and the winners will be losers. Jesus told the chief priests, "Truly I say to you that the tax collectors and prostitutes will get into the kingdom of God before you" (Matthew 21:31, NASB). Christianity is simpler and grander than the commentators and theologians have made it out to be: "Treat others the way you would have them treat you" is indeed the whole law and the prophets.

Toward the end of the story, the dream world of Don Quixote is shattered, and addlebrained Alonso Chiana is dying in his family's home. Aldonza breaks into his room. Alonso does not recognize her. He is weak and sick and confused.

"It is possible I knew you once, but I do not remember," he says.

Aldonza kneels by his bedside and pleads, "Please! Try to remember!"

"Is it so important?" he asks.

"It is everything!" she replies. "My whole life. You spoke to me and everything was...different."

"I spoke to you?" Alonso whispers.

"You called me by another name. Dulcinea...When

you spoke the name, an angel seemed to whisper, 'Dulcinea... Dulcinea...'"[9]

All the pent-up longing in the human heart of Aldonza explodes as she pours out to Alonso what happened when he called her by this name, the earthquake in her spirit caused by his love and acceptance. His calling her a "lady" awakened something in her she thought she could never be. She had been dead, frozen, immune to human emotion. The triumph of her life was not to need anyone. But he had broken into the sealed chamber of her heart, and she began to unfreeze. Seeds of hope, long buried, sprang to life. She began to believe that she was Dulcinea. Everything was different because she had been touched by the love of a dreamy old man who called himself Don Quixote.

In my study I kneel before the crucifix and see the human face of God. Throughout his passion Jesus condemned no one. Throughout his life his words were not those of blaming and shaming, accusing and condemning, threatening, bribing, and labeling. Nor should mine be.

The Crucified One looks directly at me. His eyes are so filled with blood and tears and pain, he can hardly see me. Then from his wounded heart, he whispers my name. Not any given name, no more than he calls Aldonza by her given name. It is the name of the white stone (see Revelation 2:17) by which he knows me. In the bright darkness of faith, everything is different. I sense new life throbbing within me. The name astounds me. It signifies acceptance, affirmation, tenderness, healing, and it effects what it signifies. For his word overrides my ego-evaluation. God sees everything differently. There is peace, joy, certainty, awe, and wonder. An overwhelming sense of Mystery inexpressible. I arise, knowing in the words of Paul that I am a letter from Christ written not with ink but with the Spirit of the living God, not on a stone tablet but on the fleshy tablet of my heart (see 2 Corinthians 3:3).

And at least for this one day my letter will be signed with the signature of Jesus.

Lord Jesus Christ, Son of God,
we pray that our faith-experience of you keep pace
with our credal statements about you.
Grace us with the courage to pray.
Anoint us with the spirit of compassion that we
may be with you in the passion of our times;
that we may be poor with those who are poor,
mourn with those who mourn,
enter into the struggle of our generation for social
justice, treat others as we would like to be treated.
We pray for the courage to risk everything on you,
to be with you in your faithfulness
to your mission, our mission.
For this I have come into the world, to say,
"Here I am, Lord, I come to do your will."

Chapter Three

POWER
and WISDOM

While the Jews demand miracles and the Greeks look for wisdom, we are preaching a crucified Christ: to the Jews an obstacle they cannot get over, to the gentiles foolishness, but to those who have been called, whether they are Jews or Greeks, a Christ who is both the power of God and the wisdom of God.... I was resolved that the only knowledge I would have while I was with you was knowledge of Jesus, and him as the crucified Christ.

1 CORINTHIANS 1:23−25, 2:2, NJB

*I*N FLANNERY O'CONNOR'S short story "A Good Man Is Hard to Find," the central character is an escaped convict who calls himself the Misfit "because I can't make what all I done wrong fit what all I gone through in punishment." Just before he shoots in cold blood a trembling grandmother who begs him to pray to Jesus, the Misfit utters a swift sentence, unaware of how profoundly Christian it is: "Jesus throws everything off balance."[1]

Yes, Jesus throws everything off balance. In first-century Palestine, the cross was an instrument of torture, a gallows; the honoring of anyone who hung on it was a scandal of the most profound kind. Yet in a stunning reversal of human wisdom, the cross of death becomes the Tree of Life.

Early church father John Chrysostom wrote:

> When men seek signs and wisdom and not only do not receive the things they seek, but even hear the contrary to what they seek, and then have their minds changed by these contraries, does this not show the unspeakable power of him who is preached? It's like the doctor who could win patients who had been burned and wounded and were desperately in need of medicine, by promising to cure them not with drugs, but by burning them again! This would be the result of great power indeed. So also Paul won the day, not without a sign, but by a sign that seemed contrary to all human signs—Christ crucified.[2]

Everything is off balance, indeed.

Where do we find the soul of Pauline spirituality? In ringing declarations such as "that I may know him and the power of his resurrection and partake of his sufferings by being moulded to the pattern of his death" (Philippians 3:10, NJB) and "God forbid that I should glory, save in the cross of our Lord Jesus Christ" (Galatians 6:14, KJV). To those seeking the power and wisdom of God, the signs point to the crucifixion of Jesus Christ. Such power and wisdom are more than desirable; they are crucial to living lives that are marked by the signature of Jesus.

For Paul, any spirituality that spurns the Cross, even if it leads to the heights of mystical contemplation, is utterly devoid of power and wisdom, and therefore worthless. Paul speaks not only of a crucified Christ, but of crucified men and women. Even a superficial study of church history reveals that the Spirit of God blows with hurricane force only through those prophets and lovers who have surrendered to the folly of the Cross. If there is shallow wisdom and little power in our worship and ministry, I believe it is because so few of us have gotten into the business of what Paul calls dying daily to self-centeredness in all its forms, including self-promotion and self-condemnation.

At different times in my journey, I have noticed the power and wisdom of the crucified Christ conspicuously absent from my life and ministry. How does this happen? Let me illustrate by sharing from personal experience two surefire ways guaranteed to preserve your equilibrium and protect yourself from getting thrown "off balance" by Jesus.

The first is to *intellectualize* the passion and death of Christ. This is what I was doing years ago when I was teaching Christology in graduate school. Every Monday night I surrounded myself with a bunch of good Christian folk who enjoyed the sounds of high-flown language and spirituality. The group decided to do a historical study of the efficacy of Christ's death and resurrection. One person volunteered to study Ignatius of Antioch in the second century. Another took Cyril of Jerusalem in the third, somebody else Origen and Tertullian in the fourth, another Augustine in the fifth. Then into the Dark Ages: Hugh of St. Victor and Hugh of St. Lombard. Somebody picked up Anselm in the twelfth century, another Thomas Aquinas in the thirteenth, then Martin Luther in the sixteenth. John Calvin was next, then contemporary theologians Wolfhart Pannenberg, Jürgen Moltmann, Karl Rahner, and Karl Barth.

Feeling a smug spirit of superiority over the unwashed who were caught up in Monday night football, we spoke to one another in pedantic tones about "the soteriological value" of Jesus' redemptive suffering and death. The problem with all this intellectualizing is that it allowed us to wrap the crucified Christ up in words. As we focused on our studies, we separated ourselves from his humanity. We marked him only for our minds, so there was never any pressure in our guts to change our lives.

Years ago, a prominent Christian layman told me, "Brennan, if you go around the country preaching a crucified Christ, people are going to get through before you do." He went on to point out that nobody wants to hear about Christ crucified these days. Everybody wants Jesus the agent of social change, or Christ the revolutionary, or the Master of interpersonal relationships who is going to help them win friends and influence people. But nobody wants to hear about a Christ nailed to the wood who says, "Change your life. Strike out in a new direction. Come follow me and allow yourself to be radically discipled."

In his landmark work *The Crucified God*, Jürgen Moltmann says, "We have made the bitterness of the Cross tolerable to ourselves by learning to understand it as a theological necessity for the process of salvation."[3] Of course, theological necessities do not sweat blood in the night.

Yet the Son of God did. The passion of Jesus did not take place on a cold, intellectual, starlit plain; it occurred in the deepest expression of human emotion, amid dirt and sweat, blood and tears. Christ's passionate outpouring of love on the cross is not only the source of our salvation; it is the source of God's power and wisdom in our daily lives. When we limit ourselves to intellectual speculation about Christ, we strip our lives of this power and wisdom.

A second way to deprive ourselves of power and wisdom is to *mineralize* the passion and death of Christ. By that, I mean we turn Jesus into an object: that calm, familiar naked man glued to our crucifixes. Two thousand years ago, the Son of God hung on a real cross and bled real blood; today, his lifeless image hangs from imitation crosses. On a visit to Royal Street in New Orleans, you can find reproductions of Jesus on nearly every corner. As you walk, an antique dealer might call to you, "Come, look at this! Now, the Venus costs more, but this ivory Christ is beautiful in its own way. Especially if you mount it on a velvet backdrop." As you gaze admiringly at the beautiful artwork, you might begin to see Jesus as an object to be purchased. You see, the more we reproduce Jesus, the more we forget about him and the agony of his third hour. We turn the monstrous scandal of Calvary into a piece of dignified jewelry to be worn around the neck.

Throughout the centuries, Christian artists have given the crucified Christ a rolling eye or a contorted mouth. Painters have used red lead to make realistic drops of blood flow from his hands and feet and side. Sculptors have labored with great effort to carve his body on the cross. But on that Friday two thousand years ago, the Roman soldiers carved our brother Jesus with no trouble at all. No artistic skill was required to hammer in the nails, no paint needed to make blood gush from his hands and feet and side. His mouth was contorted terribly simply by hoisting him up on a cross.

Intellectualization and *mineralization*—these are barriers that keep us from realizing the reality of the crucifixion. We have so effectively removed ourselves from the passion and death of this sacred man that we no longer see his bleeding tissue, his shattered bones, his raging thirst. On some crucifixes, Christ seems actually tranquil, especially the ones where he wears a halo. His quiet composure gives us the idea, *Ho-hum, his whole life must have been like that.*

It seems to be our natural human inclination to focus not on Christ's suffering, but on his love and the miracle of his resurrection. We desire to think about joy and not anguish. Yet recognition of Christ's pain cannot be separated from a knowledge of his love.

I was a Franciscan priest for twenty-six years. During that time, I came to understand why the founder of the community, Francis of Assisi, could never eat a meal in a room where a cross or a crucifix hung without weeping yet is remembered as the most joyful saint in Christian history. This is possible because the focus of Francis's attention was not on suffering itself, but on the *suffering Christ*. Francis knew that if he had been the only person ever to walk the earth, Jesus would have endured the shame of the Cross for him alone.

It is in this, Jesus' greatest act of love, that the power and wisdom of God are supremely manifested. This is the power and wisdom that allows us to live out the signature of Jesus in our lives. The imitation of Christ is not the imitation of a dead hero; Christ lives in the Christian, and the Christian lives in the risen Christ through the Holy Spirit. We have been empowered to live lives not ruled by selfishness and self-absorption. Yet as John McKenzie wrote, "How few Christians there are who realize they have been transformed by the power of Christ's death and that now the impossible has become possible."[4]

I would like to share what the past four decades of meditating on the crucified Christ have meant in my life. I shall speak of certain graces, or *charisms*, that are mediated most powerfully through the crucified Christ.

1. *The courage to take up the cross.* God asks each of us to accept our own "cross." Our own wounds, our own limitations, our own personality defects, the damage people have done to us from the beginning of life until today, the pain of the human condition as we have personally experienced it—this is our true cross.

For me, it is the terror of abandonment that has stalked me since I was a little boy—the frightening feeling that there is no one there for me, that I have to perform well for you to like me. In my life, it is what I believe to be the genetic predisposition to alcoholism that killed my best friend, my brother Rob, leaving behind a wife and six children. It is my own relapse with alcohol, the shivering and trembling in the detox center, the unbearable tinglies and crawlies and terrifying depression that accompany withdrawal. All this is what Christ asks me to accept and allow him to share.

For you, it may be the loss of a deeply treasured relationship. It may be the struggle to achieve success in an antagonistic work environment or a recent financial failure. It may be ongoing struggles with a rebellious teenager or unbearable loneliness stemming from rejection by your spouse. All this, and more, Christ asks you to accept and allow him to share.

In his passion and death, Jesus has experienced my pain and yours and made it his own. What happens in this encounter with the Crucified is that we enter into something that has already happened, our union with Jesus and all that it implies: his taking unto himself our pain, anxiety, fears, shame, self-hatred, and discouragement.

It is all included implicitly in his cry, "My God, My God, why have You abandoned Me?" (Matthew 27:46, AMP). His friends were scattered, his honor broken, his message torn to shreds. He stood condemned as a criminal. Yet this was the moment of our redemption. Why? Because his cry on the cross was our cry of desperate alienation from God taken up into his and transformed through the resurrection. As we allow ourselves to experience our own pain, we can know that what we feel is Christ suffering in us and redeeming us. Rather than condemning ourselves for our weakness and making self-conscious efforts to try harder, we can allow the Crucified to love us in our brokenness. There is no way of healing from the wounds each of us carries except through the love of Jesus that forgives seventy times seven and keeps no score of our wrongdoing.

2. *The willingness to forgive.* Paul wrote in Romans, "While we were still his enemies, he loved us." This is the unmistakable sign of the disciple who has actually experienced the forgiveness of Jesus: the ability to forgive his or her enemies. Jesus says, "Love your enemies and do good.… You will have a great reward, and you will be children of the Most High, for he himself is kind to the ungrateful and the wicked" (Luke 6:35, NJB).

Let me repeat: Jesus Christ crucified is not merely some heroic example to the church. He is the living power and wisdom of God empowering us to reach out a hand of healing to people who have ripped us off, screwed us up, and turned us down. As we hear him pray for his murderers, "Father, forgive them; for they know not what they do" (Luke 23:34, KJV), he slowly turns our hearts of stones into hearts of flesh. At the foot of the cross we recognize ourselves as forgiven enemies of God and are empowered to extend forgiveness and reconciliation.

Jesus' call to forgiveness is addressed not only to the wife whose husband forgot their wedding anniversary, but to the parents whose child was slaughtered by a drunken driver, to the victims of slanderous accusations, and to the poor who live in filthy boxes as the rich drive by in their Mercedes. It is extended to the sexually molested and to spouses shamed by the unfaithfulness of their partners, to believers who have been terrorized by their pastors with images of a vengeful God, to the mother in El Salvador whose daughter's body was returned to her with her head shoved into her butchered womb, to the elderly couple who lost all their savings because their bankers were thieves and gamblers, and to the woman whose alcoholic husband squandered her inheritance. It is extended to those who are the object of ridicule, discrimination, and prejudice.

Writhing in agony on the cross, Jesus says, "I know every moment of sin, selfishness, dishonesty, and degraded love that has disfigured your life, and I do not judge you unworthy of compassion, forgiveness, and salvation. Now you be like that with others. Judge no one."

Only when we claim the love of the crucified Christ with heartfelt conviction, this love that transcends all judgments, can we overcome all fear of judgment. As long as we continue to live as if we are what we do, as if we are what we have, and as if we are what other people think about us, we will remain filled with judgments, opinions, evaluations, and condemnations. We will remain addicted to the need to put people in their place.

Yet to the extent that we embrace the truth that our core identity is not rooted in our success in ministry or in our popularity with kids and parents or with power in the local church, but in the passionate, pursuing, infinite—what G. K. Chesterton called the "furious" love of God embodied in his crucified Son—to that degree we can let go of our need to judge our friends, spouses, children, pastors, gays, straights, Asians, Caucasians, and the sin-scarred wino on the street. We can be free from the need to judge others by claiming for ourselves the truth, "I am the disciple whom Jesus loves."

In the words of Henri Nouwen:

> Only when we claim the love of the crucified Christ with heartfelt conviction, the love that transcends all judgments, can we overcome all fear of judgment. When we have become completely free from the need to judge others, we will also become completely free from the fear of being judged.... The experience of not having to judge cannot co-exist with the fear of being judged, and the experience of the nonjudgmental love of the crucified Savior cannot co-exist with a need to judge others.[5]

That's what Jesus means when he says, "Do not judge, and you will not be judged" (Matthew 7:1, NJB). The apostle John, the lone male disciple who stood at the foot of the cross, says, "In love there is no room for fear" (1 John 4:18, NJB). If you are still afraid of judgment, go kneel at the cross and the Messiah will set you free.

3. The discovery of where true wisdom lies. We often think of wisdom as the sum of knowledge, insight, and learning we have accumulated in the process of living, but the wisdom I speak of here is your own existential experience of the love of Christ crucified. What is the evidence that points to the source of true wisdom? It is your own experience of release from chronic egocentricity. It is your own deliverance from chronic niceness. It is your own awareness that absolutely nothing—neither the negative judgments of others nor your debased perception of yourself; neither your scandalous past nor fear, guilt, self-loathing, or even death—can tear you away from the love of God made visible on Calvary. This is what confirms the place where wisdom resides.

A loss of faith in the power and wisdom of God, which is the love of Christ, has led to some strange aberrations in ministry. One such aberration is the idolatry of psychology. I wish to speak carefully here. I have found psychotherapy an invaluable tool in understanding myself and the world in which I live. A few years ago when Roslyn and I were struggling, two psychiatrists—one a Christian and the other a Jew—gave me enormous insight into myself and the repetitive patterns of behavior, rooted in childhood, that negatively affected my marriage. But therapy is no substitute for the gospel. Its healing power is puny compared to the power and wisdom of the crucified Lord.

Harvard psychiatrist Robert Coles asks, "Why is it that psychiatry has found so much intellectual and even moral authority among the clergy?" Coles goes on to tell what I find to be a hair-raising story about the visit of a priest to a chronically sick man in a hospital. When the priest asked, "How are you doing?" the sick man replied, "Fine," meaning that he did not want to elaborate. The priest simply would not accept that answer and insisted on a line of probing and questioning about the man's psychological state. The priest no doubt meant well, but when he left, the patient was outraged. The man had wanted to talk with the priest about God and his ways, about Christ's life and death, about heaven and salvation, only to be approached repeatedly with psychological words and phrases. In their entirety, these words and phrases constituted a statement, an insinuation: "You are in psychological jeopardy, and that is what I, an ordained priest of the Roman Catholic church, have learned to consider more important than anything else when in the presence of a person such as you."

The patient was beside himself. "He comes here with a Roman collar and offers me psychological banalities as God's Word." The priest was mesmerized by the mind and its psychological workings, but he was not alert to the man's situation in the light of eternity.

Coles concludes, "I wonder whether the muckiest mire, the deepest waters for many of America's ministers may be found in the dreary, solipsistic world so many of us have learned to find interesting: the mind's moods, the various stages and phases of human development, all dwelt upon (God save us) as if they were the stations of the Cross."

I want to say this as clearly and forcefully as I can: When I am dying, I do not want an amateur psychologist; I want a priest or minister who knows what to do. I want a man or woman who has struggled honestly with his or her faith and still clung to Jesus. I want somebody who has looked long and lovingly at Christ crucified. I want a wounded healer.

4. *The surrender of the heart to reckless love.* This is the charism so powerfully demonstrated by Mary Magdalene

and the apostle John. Throughout Jesus' agony, the focus of attention for both Mary and John was not suffering, but the suffering Christ who "loved us and gave himself up for us" (Ephesians 5:2).

Never allow these words to be interpreted as allegory. The love of Jesus Christ on the cross was a burning and divine reality for Mary and John, and their lives are utterly incomprehensible except in terms of it. Mary would have been buried in history as another tragic heroine if it were not for her immense, passionate, and uncompromising love for the person of Jesus. John would have vanished from memory as a disillusioned disciple. Yet both stood with Jesus as he was murdered in the most brutal and dehumanizing way. Jesus said of Magdalene what he said of no one else in the Gospels, though he surely says it of anyone with the spirit of Magdalene: "Her many sins have been forgiven—for she loved much" (Luke 7:47).

Should you speak to Mary and John of the Christian life, ministry, prayer, or discipleship, you must speak of Jesus nailed to the wood and now risen in glory, or not speak at all. Do not burden them with your theological insights. Do not bore them with your ministerial successes or your gift of tongues. They have only one question: "Do you know him?"

Jesus said, "Know the truth, and the truth will set you free" (John 8:32). What is the basic truth that set John and Magdalene free? It is that Christ loved them beyond worthiness and unworthiness, beyond boundary, limit, or breaking point. This greatest of all the charisms—not simply the intellectual cognition, but the experiential awareness of it—is the wisdom I am talking about, which is mediated through the spirit of the crucified Lord. As Francis de Sales said, "It is upon Calvary of Christ's cross that the saints meditate, contemplate, and come to experience their Lord."[6]

In the realm of Christian discipleship I believe the church has never had two greater lovers of Jesus Christ than Mary of Magdala and the apostle John. The personal experience of the love of Christ is the power and wisdom that illuminated, transformed, and transfigured Mary, John, and all the extravagant lovers in Christian history. The courage to take up the cross, the charism of forgiveness, and the discovery of wisdom are the Lord's legacy to those who enter deeply into the mystery of his suffering and death. The prophetic word of Jesus spoken to a thirty-four-year-old widow named Marjory Kemp almost four hundred years ago remains ever ancient, ever new: "More pleasing to me than all your prayers, sacrifices, and good words is that you would believe that I love you."

In this chapter I have focused on what Jesus' dying means for our living. The Crucified says, "Take up your cross not annually, but daily. Forgive those who hate you or hurt you, cheat you or scorn you. Reject the world-wisdom that fastens your identity on money, pleasure, power, and the psychological insights of the social sciences; find your true self in the faith-wisdom of my servant Paul: 'Christ loved us and gave himself up for us' (Ephesians 5:2)."

Is such power and wisdom within the reach of an ordinary disciple? Yes! But only if we realize that what Jesus commands, he empowers us to do. We can live the crucified lifestyle, not because we are Supermen or Wonder Women, but only because he lives in us. "I have been crucified with Christ and yet I am alive; yet it is no longer I, but Christ living in me" (Galatians 2:20, NJB).

Jesus Christ nailed to the cross is the power and wisdom of God.

He is ours as well.

Chapter Four

FOOLS
for CHRIST

$\mathcal{D}$OES THE PHRASE "A Christian is in the world but not of the world" correspond to the reality in which we live? One of the funny things about reality is its robust resistance to theories, abstractions, and ideals. The proverb "A stitch in time saves nine" does not confront procrastination, nor does the wisdom of Benjamin Franklin's "A penny saved is a penny earned" address the daily reality of the compulsive shopper.

To be "in the world but not of the world" implies that a Christian is not influenced and intimidated by the values of our American culture. Isn't that an absurd proposition? Whether we like it or not, our very membership in

Western society imprisons us in a set of political, economic, social, and spiritual principles that shape our lifestyles, even when we don't subscribe to it. Several years ago the front page of the *New York Times* showed a nine-year-old Vietnamese girl running toward us, her flesh aflame from napalm. A few years later papers printed the picture of a seven-year-old Libyan girl crawling toward a Red Cross shelter, both of her feet amputated by one of our "precision" bombs. We may weep at such sights, but our taxes buy the weapons that bring them about. I am compromised by the fact that one of the reasons for writing this book is to make money. I don't like that. But I am caught in and cultivated by our culture.

A critique of our culture in the light of the gospel is imperative if the church of Jesus Christ is to preserve a coherent sense of itself in a world that is torn and tearing. To criticize the system of Western technological capitalism is neither unpatriotic nor un-American, for as Walter Wink, professor of biblical interpretation at Auburn Theological Seminary in New York City, noted, "We cannot minister to the soul of America unless we love its soul."[1] A chastened patriotism is indispensable for the survival of the nation as well as of the church. National attitudes and policies change only because people love their country.

I see three areas where the American Dream is counter-evangelical—that is, in direct opposition to the message of Jesus and a life endorsed with the signature of Jesus. Our culture, as John Kavanaugh observed, "fosters and sustains a functional trinitarian god of consumerism, hedonism, and nationalism. Made in the image and likeness of such a god, we are committed to lives of possessiveness, pleasure, and domination."[2]

Unless the church of the Lord Jesus creates a counter-current to the drift of materialism, self-indulgence, and nationalism, Christians will merely adapt to the secular environment in a tragic distortion of the gospel, in which the words of Jesus are reinterpreted to mean anything, everything, and nothing.

One school of thought, for example, assures us that the New Testament is filled with Oriental exaggerations, that Jesus never intended us to take the gospel literally—we have merely projected our mechanistic Western mentality on the poetic, Semitic thought patterns of Christ. After all, no one can have a plank of wood in his eye! And what about that impossible image in Matthew 19:24, "It is easier for a camel to go through the eye of a needle than for a rich man to enter the kingdom of God"? Such language is not only impossible but offensive. Look at the good money can do! Even Christian undertakings must be financed. And those images of the woman in labor found in John and the emptying of the bowels in Mark—the language is too strong. It is more prudent to render these dangerous maxims harmless. Pour as much water as possible into the fiery wine of Christ.

Such reductionisms dilute the radical demands of discipleship so that Jesus is frequently honored today for what he did *not* mean rather than for what he *did* mean. An unthinking, uncritical cultural propaganda becomes more persuasive than the sayings of Jesus regarding what is real, true, good, and of enduring value.

Jesus' summons to simplicity of life, in fact, lies in diametric opposition to the consumerism of our culture. An article in *People* magazine quoted Charlie Sheen, star of the Oscar-winning films *Wall Street* and *Platoon*, as saying, "Money is energy, man." The article notes that on the downstairs sofa of Sheen's apartment are five remote control devices for various video and audio components. Upstairs he has an office equipped with the latest computer and gym equipment. "I'm the definition of decadence," Sheen says.

An article in *Time* magazine was devoted to shopping addicts. One man explained that he had no time to waste making choices, so he bought twenty pairs of shoes at Bloomingdale's. "Possession is the whole point. I like seeing the stuff around me like a security blanket."

An issue of *Newsweek* carried a report on the formation of tomorrow's consumers: "Toymakers and animation houses now build entire kidvid shows around planned or existing lines of playthings. The programs become, in effect, little more than half-hour commercials for their toycasts."

The relentless bombardment of the media on children to buy, want, and consume prompted Thomas Merton to write:

> The modern child may early in his or her existence have natural inclinations toward spirituality. The child may have imagination, originality, a simple and individual response to reality, and even a tendency to moments of thoughtful silence and

absorption. All these tendencies, however, are soon destroyed by the dominant culture. The child becomes a yelling, brash, false little monster, brandishing a toy gun or dressed up like some character he has seen on television. His head is filled with inane slogans, songs, noises, explosions, statistics, brand names, menaces, ribaldries, and cliches. Then, when the child gets to school, he learns to verbalize, rationalize, to pace, to make faces like an advertisement, to need a car and in short, to go through life with an empty head conforming to others, like himself, in togetherness.[3]

We Americans are programmed to be consumers. Here in New Orleans, after the collapse of the oil and gas business, we were in the throes of a deep recession for several years. Yet when a new multimillion-dollar shopping complex named the Riverwalk opened with celebrity fanfare, we were deluged with radio and TV ads, highway billboards, and flyers on our doorsteps, urging us to bring our checkbooks and credit cards to the ribbon-cutting gala. Even when hard-pressed financially, we are pressured by our culture to consume. This is our identity.

Polls reveal that the making of money has become the dominant aspiration of students entering college. In a survey of ten thousand high school students in New Jersey, 89 percent wanted to make a lot of money, while 11 percent wanted positions of power. None wanted to be holy.

The insistence of Jesus on simplicity of life is un-American. Acceptance of the gospel lifestyle would mean disaster for business. Several years ago I had the opportunity to visit Wall Street. For three days I observed the frenzy in the pit (where stocks are traded) and the commodities exchange where elbowing, shoving, and aggressive jockeying for position are accepted etiquette. Though there are several prayer groups in the Wall Street area where Christian businessmen and women try to relate the Word to the market, I left with the impression that the pursuit of wealth is esteemed as the supreme good of life.

Are we people of God in the world but not *of* the world? Or are we more capitalistic than Christian? Our culture blasphemously implies that the bottom line is really the bottom line. Church ministries are evaluated by the size of their budgets. Retirement is anxiously discussed in monetary terms. We are impressed by wealth. We go to great lengths to stand well with the moneyed and prosperous. A person's worth is measured by the dollars he or she generates. Money assumes a spiritual dimension. Stature in the community is determined by the size and geographical location of one's home, the quality of the automobile, and the array of trinkets, gadgets, and creature comforts one has collected.

The prosperity gospel is but one feeble attempt to accommodate the sayings of Jesus to our consumer culture. The words of Jesus—"Do not store up for yourselves treasure on earth"; "Do not worry about tomorrow"; "You cannot serve both God and Money"—seem alien to most of us struggling to meet mortgage, car, and tuition payments. The cultural propaganda embodied in two liquor advertisements, "Living well is the best revenge" and "Sip it with arrogance," have a curious, perhaps demonic appeal. Consumerism indeed has its own spirituality.

Perhaps the darkest dimension to the accumulation of wealth is the exploitation of cheap labor to procure the luxuries we've grown used to. If you had a cup of coffee this morning, as I did, you participated: "In Africa a healthy young adult male cannot possibly make more than $1.50 a day picking coffee. It is no wonder that women and children are compelled to share in the picking."[4] If we paid the East African pickers the minimum American wage, we could not afford to drink the coffee.

Let us be bold enough to ask ourselves, as Christians, whether the church of the Lord Jesus in the United States has anything to say to our nation and its ideologies of materialism, possessiveness, and the worship of financial security. Are we courageous enough to be a sign of contradiction to consumerism through our living faith in Jesus Christ? Are we committed enough to his gospel to become a counter-current to the drift? Or have we so accommodated the faith of our fathers to consumption that the question of simplicity of life, sharing of resources, and radical dependence on God's providence no longer seem relevant? How do we build the kingdom of God on earth if what we incarnate in our lives is the dogma of our culture rather than the revelation of Jesus? Where is the signature of Jesus?

The second area of American culture in opposition to the gospel is hedonism versus purity of heart. Lead guitarist Slash of the rock band Guns N' Roses has said, "We're very close to the kids we play for. That's what rock 'n' roll is for me, a kind of rebellious thing, getting away from authority figures, getting laid, getting drunk, doing drugs at some point."

A few years ago, a San Antonio radio station asked young fans what they would do to meet a rock band called Mötley Crüe. One thirteen-year-old girl said, "I'd do it with the Crüe, till black and blue is all you see..."

A media analyst has noted that television viewers watch more incidences of intercourse between strangers than between married people.[5]

Scripture scholar John McKenzie has said, "The basis of Western civilization is the amassing of wealth through the exploitation of nature."[6] And that includes human nature. Today's Top 40 music spawns a hedonism that makes promiscuity the norm. Marketing success makes anything acceptable, including providing condoms for one-night stands with vulnerable teenagers. The awesome power of money to legitimize sexual immorality in our culture seeds ambiguity and confusion among churchgoers as much as anywhere else.

I am told, and I am sure you have been told, that I'm living in the Stone Age if I suggest that promiscuity or marital infidelity is unacceptable in the life of a disciple of Jesus Christ. Should you proclaim with Paul that the body is for the Lord and the Lord for the body, that you are not your own property, that you have been bought and paid for with the blood of Christ, that your body is a temple of the Holy Spirit, you will be subject to mockery and derision. "At our annual shareholders meeting in Las Vegas each year," a businessman told me, "the sexual behavior of Christians is no different from that of unbelievers. And why not? Everybody has a good time and nobody gets hurt."

The third area of American culture in conflict with the gospel is domination through violence. In his inaugural address, the Sermon on the Mount, Jesus declared, "Blessed are the peacemakers, for they will be called sons of God" (Matthew 5:9). The question of peace in a violent world is so important that I do not believe anyone who takes the Christian faith seriously can afford to neglect it. I am not suggesting that you have to swim out to a Trident submarine with a banner between your teeth, but it is necessary to take a serious and articulate stand on nuclear war. And I mean against nuclear war. The passivity, the indifference of many Christians on the issue and, worse still, the active belligerence of some religious spokesmen, is becoming one of the most frightful scandals in the history of Christendom. The church must proclaim that Western civilization "will escape the ultimate horror only by attending to the person and the words of Jesus Christ. Like Paul, that is all we have to say; so for Christ's sake let us say it."[7]

"Syndicated columnist Jeffrey Hart suggested that the president give a speech with this ending paragraph: 'In the future, and on principle, we guarantee that we will retaliate for the death or injury of a U.S. citizen at the ratio of 500 to 1. As I speak to you, I have received word that fifteen Shiite villages and their inhabitants no longer exist.'"[8]

Jeffrey Hart is a Christian. I find his words profoundly disturbing. We are a nation that calls itself a believing people, but which lives in disobedience to the will of God. It is this vengeful spirit, so contrary to the gospel, that reminds me of Mark Twain's famous *War Prayer*, in which he skewered the hypocrisy of Christians:

> O Lord our Father, our young patriots, idols of our hearts, go forth to battle—be Thou near them! With them, in spirit, we also go forth from the sweet peace of our beloved firesides to smite the foe! Lord our God, help us to tear their soldiers to bloody shreds with our shells; help us to cover their smiling fields with the pale forms of their patriot dead; help us to drown the thunder of the guns with the shrieks of their wounded, writhing in pain; help us to lay waste their humble homes with a hurricane of fire; help us to wring the hearts of their unoffending widows [and leave them and] their little children to wander unfriended the wastes of their desolated land in rags and hunger and thirst, sports of the sun flames of summer and the icy winds of winter, broken in spirit, worn with travail, imploring Thee for the refuge of the grave and denied it—for our sakes who adore Thee, Lord, blast their hopes, blight their lives, protract their bitter pilgrimage, make heavy their steps, water their way with tears, stain the white snow with the blood of their wounded feet! We ask it, in the spirit of Love, of Him who is the Source of Love, and Who is the ever-faithful refuge and friend of all that are sore beset and seek His aid with humble and contrite hearts. Amen.[9]

As in Twain's day we continue to confuse nationalized faith with fidelity to Jesus Christ. Jingoism and Christianity become synonymous in the belief that God is pleased with, beholden to, partial to, and identified with our land. Such was the rationale behind the atomic destruction of Hiroshima and Nagasaki that vaporized a couple hundred thousand civilian noncombatants in order to "save American lives."

"The willingness of the majority of believers to accept the nuclear bomb, with all that it implies, with no more than a shadow of theoretical protest, is almost unbelievable, and yet it has become so commonplace that no one wonders at it anymore."[10] The pragmatic wisdom of "self-defense" and "national security" masks our childish fantasies of revenge, where we can devastate the enemy in such a way that there is no possibility of retaliation. Our Clint Eastwoods, our subway vigilantes populate our dreams, our prayers, and our illusions. A Christian is in the world but not of the world?

Ernest Becker, in his book *Escape from Evil*, has remarked that one way we escape from evil is to project it onto others. So we become a fierce nation toppling foreign governments at will for "good and noble" reasons. The method for establishing domination is not reverence but violence. "And although we give lip service to Jesus, we give every other kind of service to Caesar and Mars [the god of war]."[11]

The spirit of domination through force is irreconcilable with obedience to the gospel of Jesus Christ.

Christians have only one master. Following him is incompatible with any state of servitude to any other. Jesus couched his teachings in language that any twelve-year-old can understand. He said unequivocally, blessed are those who make peace, not war. The issue of the production, possession, and use of nuclear weapons must be discussed in terms of our Christian identity, not in terms of national security, the Iraqi threat, or safeguarding our standard of living. The arms race is not a political football but a deeply spiritual matter. Mass murder in the name of democracy or patriotism is the idolatry of the nation-state. The prophetic task and pastoral obligation of the church of Jesus Christ—a people called together, set apart, and consecrated to the worship of God—is to proclaim God's peace and love in the actual situation of our broken and tormented world.

Calling peacemakers "bleeding hearts," "do-gooders," and "good Samaritans" with a tone of condescension indicates an unacknowledged alienation from the gospel. When will Christians be honest enough to admit that they don't really believe in Jesus Christ? That the Nazarene carpenter must be dismissed as a romantic visionary, a starry-eyed reformer hopelessly out of touch with the "real" world of domination, aggression, and power? Only when they realize that they have embraced their culture as their false god!

If Christian men and women are to live the gospel today in our post-industrial American culture, if we are to be in the world and not of the world, then we must be willing to assume personal responsibility for the ways in which our faith has been accommodated to possessiveness, pleasure, and domination. And we must be willing to repent, reform, and be renewed.

The church is the living extension of Jesus Christ in time and space. It is countercurrent to the drift into cultural idolatry. The church in American society today is, of necessity, a community of resistance to the gods of modern life—nuclear stockpiling, money, ego, sexual muscle, racism, pride of place. We are the pilgrim people of God with no lasting city here on earth, a community of free men and women whose freedom is not limited by the frontiers of a world that is itself in chains.

Albert Camus once said, "The only way to deal with an unfree world is to become so absolutely free that your very act of existence is an act of rebellion." There is nothing more maddening to the world than a free man or woman in Christ Jesus. People must not look to the church to reinforce the values of their culture, or to dust off on Sunday morning the idols they have been living by during the week.

The early church was built on small groups of people who came together to support one another in a whole new way of life. These primitive communities were visible evidence of an alternative to the status quo of their culture. Today we need small bands of people who take the gospel at face value, who realize what God is doing in our time, and who are living proof of what it means to be in the world but not of the world. These "base" communities or neighborhood churches should be small enough for intimacy, kindred enough for acceptance, and gentle enough for criticism. Gathered in the name of Jesus, the community empowers us to incarnate in our lives what we believe in our hearts and proclaim with our lips.

Of course, we must not romanticize such groups. It is all too easy to envision a cozy, harmonious little fellowship where everyone is tuned in on the same wavelength, to love the dream of community more than the sin-scarred members who comprise it, to fantasize heroic deeds for the Lord, and to hear the applause in heaven and on earth as we shape an angelic *koinonia*.

The reality is otherwise. Egos collide, personalities conflict, power brokers intrude, anger and resentment surface, risk is inevitable. "It is less like utopia than a crucible or refiner's fire."[12]

The experience of community is neither a luxury for the spiritually affluent nor a panacea for the lonely, bored, and idle. It is, in fact, a necessity for every Christian. It is my personal conviction that this is what Jesus and Paul meant when they spoke of the church—small Christian communities praying and worshiping together, healing, forgiving, reconciling, supporting, challenging, and encouraging one another. Scott Peck says, "There can be no vulnerability without risk; there can be no community without vulnerability; there can be no peace—and ultimately no life—without community."[13]

We need a group of people around us who support and understand us. Even Jesus needed this. He called them "the Twelve," the first Christian community. We need perspective on the present, so we pray together; we need accountability, so we share our lives with each other; we need a vision of the future, so we dream together.

And our dreams are not mere wishful thinking; rather they are charged with hope and promise because the crucified, risen Jesus has prevailed over every principality, power, and dominion. He has unmasked their illusions, exposed their lies, shown them for what they are. The risen Christ stands free from their threats and control. In union with him we conquer consumerism, hedonism, and nationalism by the power of God's love. We confront the world's powers—political tyranny, economic oppression, the nuclear meltdown—not merely with our own strength, resources, and resistance, but with the very life of the risen Christ, knowing that things impossible with men are possible with God (see Luke 18:27).

Naturally the countercultural lifestyle—simplicity of life, purity of heart, and obedience to the gospel—will take us to the same place that it took Jesus: the Cross. All roads lead to Calvary, for we preach Jesus Christ crucified—a stumbling block to Jews, an absurdity to Gentiles; but to those who are called, Christ the power and the wisdom of God.

Simplicity, purity, and obedience to the Word will leave us weak and powerless in the world's eyes because we no longer can call upon our possessions and privileged positions as security. We will be subject to derision and outrage because authentic discipleship is a life of sublime madness. Injury and insult are promised to those who labor for the sake of righteousness. Paul's word to the Galatians is utter folly to our American culture: "God forbid that I should glory, save in the cross of our Lord Jesus Christ, by whom the world is crucified unto me, and I unto the world" (Galatians 6:14, KJV).

A Christian living in the world but not of the world is a sign of contradiction to the compromises that many within the church have settled for. The disciple of Jesus will be made to look and feel like a fool. Yet fools for Christ formed the early Church. And as that tiny band of believers grew, the world witnessed the power in such foolishness.

"That same foolishness is the only hope we have of breaking free. The greatest threat to any system is the existence of fools who do not believe in the ultimate reality of that system. To repent and believe in a new reality—that is the essence of conversion."[14] We join the church whose purpose is to make visible this new reality in the world.

True disciples see Christianity as a way of life on and off camera. Obviously, it will not appeal to everyone. The ranks of church membership will be thinned. Christians will look differently and act differently from other people because they are different. The name of Jesus no longer will be mouthed casually or the Christian mysteries profaned. The scandals that recently have rocked the body of Christ will be seen in perspective as a "purifying dawn" heralding the daylight of lived faith in the living God.

Easter morning vindicated the way of Jesus and validated the authority of his lordship. The Master told us never to underestimate the power of our culture. Our world, full of incredible foolishness, will insist that we are the fools. Yet Easter convinces us of God's wisdom and his power to transform our world. Our faith in the risen Jesus is the power that overcomes ourselves, our culture, and our world.

In the words of Paul in Romans 12:2, "Do not conform any longer to the pattern of this world, but be transformed by the renewing of your mind. Then you will be able to test and approve what God's will is—his good, pleasing and perfect will."

Chapter Five

DISCIPLESHIP TODAY

*I*N JANUARY 1987 the postman delivered to me an invitation from the United States Senate and House of Representatives to attend the National Prayer Breakfast at the Washington Hilton with the president and Mrs. Reagan and other government leaders. I was asked to speak at two dinners on the night preceding the breakfast and at two seminars the following morning.

My wife, Roslyn, read the invitation and remarked, "Brennan, I knew you when you were nothin'." Simone, eighteen, and Nicole, sixteen, were heading out the door to school. Simone said, "You're still nothin'." And Nicole added, "You'll never amount to nothin'."

A Russian *starets* once said, "If you pray for humility, be careful. Humility is learned through humiliations."

What caught my eye on the invitation was a quote from Francis of Assisi. In "Letters to Rulers of People," he wrote:

> Keep a clear eye toward life's end. Do not forget your purpose and destiny as God's creature. What you are in his sight is what you are and nothing more. Remember that when you leave this earth, you can take with you nothing that you have received—fading symbols of honor, trappings of power—but only what you have given: a full heart enriched by honest service, love, sacrifice, and courage.

For Francis, discipleship, or the following of Christ, was not simply the most important thing in life—it was the only thing. It was literally a matter of eternal life and death: *I am what I am in God's sight and nothing more.* Discipleship demands that we put aside all nonessentials, stop playing word games, and come to the essence of things.

The essence for the follower of Jesus lies in living by faith and not by religion. Living by faith consists in constantly redefining and reaffirming our identity with Jesus, measuring ourselves against him—not measuring *him* against our church dogmas and local heroes. Jesus is the light of the world. In his light we discover that it is not mere rhetoric that Jesus demands but personal renewal, fidelity to the Word, and creative conduct. As Emile Leger said when he left his mansion in Montreal to go live in a leper colony in Africa, "The time for talking is over."

Religiosity per se is not discipleship; in fact, it may be a safe refuge from the revolutionary lifestyle proposed by Jesus. In October 1917, the Russian Revolution was launched and history was given a new dimension. "The story goes that that very month the Russian Orthodox Church was assembled in Council. A passionate debate was in progress about the color of the surplice to be used in liturgical functions. Some insisted vehemently that it had to be white. Others, with equal vehemence, that it had to be purple. Nero fiddled while Rome burnt."[1] Coming to grips with a revolution, Anthony DeMello comments, is infinitely more bothersome than organizing a beautiful liturgy. I'd rather say my prayers than get involved in neighborhood quarrels.

On New Year's Eve, a sincere "Christian" may decide the time has come to live like a disciple, so he or she resolves the following: I am going to get into the Word every day, join a prayer group, find a spiritual guide, do more spiritual reading, go to church more often, increase my devotional time, experiment with fasting, and shout, "Praise the Lord!" upon awakening and retiring. Many disciples do these things, yet do not follow Jesus. Though unmistakably religious, they never have submitted to the signed lifestyle.

What is the relationship between discipleship and religious practices? The latter sustain the Christian life. It is impossible to keep Christian values in focus if we do not read Scripture and pray and lean on others for support and direction. Our culture—which panders to appetite, curiosity, and distraction—and the media—which scratches our itch for possessions—otherwise will prove too strong for us.

> We need reminders, symbols, stories, exhortations, living models, time-outs for reflection and celebration. These things are indispensable supports. The error is to think these things are the Christian life. Just as Jesus' practice of prayer was in the service of a whole way of life, a means rather than an end, so must ours be. Insofar as prayer, reading, sacraments, and spiritual direction support genuine Christian living, that is, Christian attitudes, relationships, choices, and actions, they are useful. When they become an escape from the more difficult demands of Christian living, they are the corruption of discipleship. The question at the Last Judgment is not "How religious was your talk?" nor "How much time did you spend in prayer?" nor "Was your faith orthodox in every respect?" but "How did you respond to needy brothers and sisters?" This is the one reliable measure of discipleship.[2]

In preparing to write this book, I contacted several Christian communities throughout the United States, seeking their understanding of discipleship. The answers were varied, illuminating, and often profound. Combining their insights with my own (and aware of my preferences, prejudices, and partial grasp of truth) I shall focus on three features of Jesus' life and teaching and their immediate importance for discipleship today.

Jesus lived for God. The central theme in the personal life of Jesus of Nazareth was his growing intimacy with, trust in, and love for his Father. His inner life was centered on God. For him the Father meant everything. The will of the Father was the air that he breathed. "I tell you the truth, the Son can do nothing by himself; he can do only what he sees his Father doing, because whatever the Father does the Son also does" (John 5:19). The Father's will was a river of life, a bloodstream from which Jesus drew life more profoundly than from his mother. "Whoever does the will of my Father in heaven is my brother and sister and mother" (Matthew 12:50). He lived secure in his Father's acceptance. "As the Father has loved me, so have I loved you" (John 15:9).

Living for God finds its foremost expression in prayer. The heart of discipleship lies in commitment and worship, not reflection and theory. The Spirit of Jesus provides a way for us to live on the surface and out of the depths at the same time. On the surface we can think, dialogue, plan, and be fully present to the demands of the daily routine. Simultaneously and deeply within, we can be in prayer, adoration, thanksgiving, and attentiveness to the Spirit. The secret places of the heart become a sanctuary of praise in the noisy playpen of the marketplace. What masters of the interior life recommend is the discipline of "centering down" throughout the day—a quiet, persistent turning to God while driving, cooking, conversing, writing, and so on. After weeks and months of practice, relapses, discouragement, and returns to the center, this discipline becomes a habit. Brother Lawrence called it "the practice of the presence of God."

Herein lies the secret, I believe, of the inner life of Jesus. Christ's communion with Abba in the inner sanctuary of his soul transformed his vision of reality, enabling him to perceive God's love and care behind the complexities of life. Practicing the presence of God helps us to discern the providence of God at work, especially in those dark hours when the signature of Jesus is being traced in our flesh. (You may wish to try it right now. Lower the book, center down, and offer yourself to the indwelling Spirit of God.)

"If anyone loves me, he will obey my teaching. My Father will love him, and we will come to him and make our home with him" (John 14:23). In muffled cries of praise, disciples turn humbly to this indwelling God throughout the day. They are alert to the outer world of sound, sense, and meaning—this is not a discipline in absent-mindedness. They walk and talk, work and play, laugh and cry in full presence to tasks and persons. Behind the scenes, the rhythm of prayer and interior worship continues. A cry of thanksgiving is their last word before falling asleep and their first upon awakening.

The frequent repetition of the name "Jesus" or "Abba, Father" throughout the day will prove helpful. Even a mechanical recitation of the name will suffice—eventually, it gets into your subconscious and a transformation of mind and heart takes place.

The early days of this discipline are awkward, painful, and rewarding. Awkward because it requires vigilance and discipline. Painful because the lapses and relapses are frequent. (When we slip and forget God's presence within, it is self-defeating to spend time in regrets and self-condemnation. We begin anew right where we are; offer this broken worship to Jesus Christ, and thank him for the grace to center down once again.) Finally, it is rewarding because life lived in the inner sanctuary is the abundant life that Jesus promised.

Philosopher William James said, "In some people religion exists as a dull habit, in others as an acute fever." Jesus did not endure the shame of the cross to pass on a dull habit. (If you don't have the fever, dear reader, a passion for God and his Christ, drop this book, fall on your knees, and beg for it. Turn to the God you half-believe in and cry out for his baptism of fire.)

The fifteenth-century mystic Meister Eckhart wrote, "There are plenty of Christians to follow the Lord halfway, but not the other half. They will give up possessions, friends, and honors, but it touches them too closely to disown themselves." Eckhart's words touch a nerve and go to the heart of this chapter on discipleship. I am not speaking of plunging ourselves into a series of spiritual activities or lengthening the time of formal prayer or getting involved in more church-related organizations. I am not speaking of fasts, rituals, devotions, liturgies, or prayer meetings. I am speaking of a life lived completely for God, the astonishing life of a committed disciple who is willing to follow Jesus the other half. A life of surrender without reservation. I propose it in humility and boldness. I mean this literally and completely. I mean it for you and me.

To be like Christ is to be a Christian.

There is a revolutionary explosiveness to this proposal. When a disciple lives his or her life wholly for God, walking hand in hand with the Jesus for whom God is everything, the limitless power of the Holy Spirit is unleashed. God breaks through, miracles occur, the world is renewed, and history is changed. Disciples the world over, living in the light who is Christ, know with clarity that abortion and nuclear weapons are but two sides of the same hot coin minted in hell, that Christians stand upright beside the Prince of Peace and refuse to fall prostrate before the shrine of national security, that we are a life-giving and not a death-dealing people of God, that we live under the sign of the Cross and not the sign of the bomb. In the coming years, there is nothing more important than to see the human race endowed with a community of authentic disciples who, like the one they follow, live entirely for God.

To this extraordinary life of discipleship, Jesus calls us. Not as a lovely ideal, but as a serious, concrete, and realistic program of life to be lived here and now by you and me.

This is something radically different from the mild, conventional religion which, with respectable skirts held back by dirty fingers, tries to fish the world out of the sinkhole of its own selfishness. Our churches are full of such amiable and respectable people. We have plenty of Christians to follow Jesus the first half of the way. Many of us have become as half-heartedly and conventionally religious as were the church folk of two thousand years ago, against whose mildness, mediocrity, and passionlessness Jesus Christ and his disciples flung themselves with all the passion of a glorious new discovery and with all the energy of builders of the kingdom of God on earth.

A life lived for God is remarkably well rounded. Its joys are genuine, its peace profound, its humility deep, its power formidable, its love enveloping, its simplicity that of a trusting child. It is the life and power in which the prophets and apostles moved. It is the life and power of Jesus of Nazareth who taught that when the eye is single, the whole body is full of light.[3]

It is the life and power of the apostle Paul, who resolved not to know anything save Jesus Christ and him crucified. It is the life and power of Francis of Assisi, who relived the gospel more closely than any person since apostolic times. It is the life and power of countless unknown saints throughout the ages. It is the life and power of many readers of this book who nod with recognition as they read. It is the life and power that can break forth in our tottering Western culture, renew the body of Christ, and build the new heavens and the new earth.

To those disciples wishing to live their lives wholly for God, I recommend praying the Lord's Prayer three times each day—in the morning, at noon, and in the evening. This recommendation may sound too simplistic for a generation working so hard at prayer, groping in the dark for its mystic edges. We never have given up entirely our efforts to improve on the way Jesus told us to pray. We have made prayers fancier, longer, and sometimes more dramatic, but we never have made them as deep as the Lord's Prayer. In days past people fasted and kept vigil in hope of trapping the Holy Spirit; now we hold symposiums, workshops, and seminars on prayer in the same quest. We never have finished the search for something more than the staples of life that Jesus underscores in the prayer to the Father.

The devout Jew prayed the *Shema* three times daily. This prayer, found in Deuteronomy 6:4–5, reads, "Hear, O Israel: The LORD our God, the LORD is one. Love the LORD your God with all your heart and with all your soul and with all your strength." This prayer was a badge of the Jews, a sign of belonging to God's chosen people. It consecrated them to the service of Yahweh, and failure to pray it separated them from the covenant. The Jews gloried in the fact that God had revealed his name as Yahweh to them alone.

Christians glory in the truth that Jesus has revealed to them alone the name of God as Abba. The Lord's Prayer is the Christian Shema. Three times daily, it is a joyful renewal of our baptism into Christ Jesus and our initiation into the church.

Godfrey Diekmann recommends that each time we pray the Lord's Prayer we pay special attention to the petition "Forgive us our trespasses as we forgive those who trespass against us." Diekmann says, "The pagans marveled at the early Christian community saying, 'See how they love one another!' Is it possible that the Lord's Prayer prayed three times a day deliberately, conscious of its basic implication, was a major formative factor in gaining that reputation for the early Christians?"

The second major feature of Jesus' life: *Jesus lived for others*. He was not simply called but actually was the friend of publicans and sinners. He befriended the rabble, the riffraff of his own culture. "One of the mysteries of the gospel tradition is this strange attraction of Jesus to the unattractive, his strange desire for the undesirable, his strange love for the unlovely. The key to this mystery is, of course, the Father. Jesus does what he sees the Father doing, he loves those whom the Father loves."[4]

The gentleness of Jesus with sinners flowed from his ability to read their hearts and to detect the sincerity and goodness there. Behind men's grumpiest poses and most puzzling defense mechanisms, behind their arrogance and airs, behind their sneers and curses, Jesus saw little children who hadn't been loved enough and who had ceased growing because someone had ceased believing in them. Perhaps it was his extraordinary sensitivity and compassion that caused Jesus (and later the apostles) to speak of the faithful as "children," no matter how tall, rich, clever, and successful they might be.

When Jesus tied a towel around his waist, poured water into a copper basin, and washed the feet of the apostles (the dress and duty were those of a slave), the Maundy Thursday revolution began, and a new idea of greatness in the kingdom of God emerged. Jesus is Servant, ministering to the needs of others: "But if I, your teacher and Lord, have washed your feet, you must be ready to wash one another's feet. I have given you this as an example so that you may do as I have done" (John 13:14–15, Phillips).

What a shocking reversal of our culture's priorities and values! To prefer to be the servant rather than the lord of the household; to merrily taunt the gods of power, prestige, honor, and recognition; to refuse to take oneself seriously; to live without gloom by a lackey's agenda—these are the attitudes and actions that bear the stamp of authentic discipleship. In effect, Jesus said, blessed are you if you love to be unknown and regarded as nothing. All things being equal, to prefer contempt to honor, to prefer ridicule to praise, to prefer humiliation to glory—these are formulas of greatness in the kingdom of God.

So central is Jesus' teaching on humble apprenticeship and serving love as the essence of discipleship, that Christ makes himself recognizable only in our brothers and sisters: "Whatever you did for one of the least of these brothers of mine, you did for me" (Matthew 25:40). In this context, the words of Mother Teresa are impressive. At the dedication of a hospice for the terminally ill in New York City, she said, "Each AIDS victim is Jesus in a distressing disguise."

Jesus' ministry of service is rooted in his compassion for the lost, lonely, and broken. Why does he love losers, failures, those on the margin of social respectability? Because the Father does.

Charlie Brown says, "I love humanity. It's people I can't stand." In Jesus' life and teaching, it is the flesh-and-blood person, not the generality, who is to be treated with compassion—the person there in front of me, not the abstraction.

Dominique Voillaume has influenced my life as few people ever have. One New Year's morning in Saint-Remy, France, seven of us in the community of the Little Brothers of Jesus were seated at a table in an old stone house. We were living an uncloistered, contemplative life among the poor, with the days devoted to manual labor and the nights wrapped in silence and prayer.

The breakfast table talk grew animated when our discussion turned to our daily employment. A German brother remarked that our wages were substandard (sixty cents per hour). I commented that our employers never were seen in the parish church on Sunday morning. A French brother suggested that this showed hypocrisy. A Spanish brother said they were rude and greedy. The tone grew more caustic and the salvos got heavier. We concluded that our avaricious bosses were nasty, self-centered cretins who slept all day Sunday and never once lifted their minds and hearts in thanksgiving to God.

Dominique sat at the end of the table. Throughout our harangue he never opened his mouth. I glanced down the table and saw tears rolling down his cheeks. "What's the matter, Dominique?" I asked. His voice was barely audible. All he said was, *"Ils ne comprennent pas."* They don't understand! How many times since that New Year's morning has that single sentence of his turned resentment of mine into compassion? How often have I reread the passion story of Jesus in the Gospels through the eyes of Dominique Voillaume, seen Jesus in the throes of his death agony, beaten and bullied, scourged and spat upon, saying, "Father, forgive them, *ils ne comprennent pas*."

The following year, Dominique, a lean, muscular six feet, two inches, always wearing a navy blue beret, learned at age fifty-four that he was dying of inoperable cancer. With the community's permission he moved to a poor neighborhood in Paris and took a job as night watchman at a factory. Returning home every morning at 8:00 A.M. he would go directly to a little park across the street from where he lived and sit down on a wooden bench. Hanging around the park were marginal people—drifters, winos, "has-beens," dirty old men who ogled the girls passing by.

Dominique never criticized, scolded, or reprimanded them. He laughed, told stories, shared his candy, accepted them just as they were. From living so long out of the inner sanctuary, he gave off a peace, a serene sense of self-possession and a hospitality of heart that caused cynical young men and defeated old men to gravitate toward him like bacon toward eggs. His simple witness lay in accepting others as they were without questions and allowing them to make themselves at home in his heart. Dominique was the most nonjudgmental person I have ever known. He loved with the heart of Jesus Christ.

One day, when the ragtag group of rejects asked him to talk about himself, Dominique gave them a thumbnail description of his life. Then he told them with quiet conviction that God loved them tenderly and stubbornly, that Jesus had come for rejects and outcasts just like themselves. His witness was credible because the Word was enfleshed on his bones. Later one old-timer said, "The dirty jokes, vulgar language, and leering at girls just stopped."

One morning Dominique failed to appear on his park

bench. The men grew concerned. A few hours later, he was found dead on the floor of his cold-water flat. He died in the obscurity of a Parisian slum.

Dominique Voillaume never tried to impress anybody, never wondered if his life was useful or his witness meaningful. He never felt he had to do something great for God. He did keep a journal. It was found shortly after his death in the drawer of the nightstand by his bed. His last entry is one of the most astonishing things I have ever read:

> All that is not the love of God has no meaning for me. I can truthfully say that I have no interest in anything but the love of God which is in Christ Jesus. If God wants it to, my life will be useful through my word and witness. If he wants it to, my life will bear fruit through my prayers and sacrifices. But the usefulness of my life is his concern, not mine. It would be indecent of me to worry about that.

In Dominique Voillaume I saw the reality of a life lived entirely for God and for others. After an all-night prayer vigil by his friends, he was buried in an unadorned pine box in the backyard of the Little Brothers' house in Saint-Remy. A simple wooden cross over his grave with the inscription "Dominique Voillaume, a witness to Jesus Christ" said it all. More than seven thousand people gathered from all over Europe to attend his funeral.

Any spirituality that does not lead from a self-centered to an other-centered mode of existence is bankrupt. For many of us the journey out of preoccupation with self begins with self-acceptance. In order to live for others I must be able to live with myself. Years ago the Swiss psychologist Carl Jung asked:

> What if I should discover that the least of the brothers of Jesus, the one crying out most desperately for reconciliation, forgiveness, and acceptance, is myself? That I myself stand in need of the alms of my own kindness, that I myself am the enemy who must be loved, what then? Will I do for myself what I do for others?

My own need for self-acceptance singed my conscience in the terminal of the Kansas City airport. I was en route from Clearwater, Florida, to Des Moines, Iowa, to lead a retreat. Bad weather rerouted my plane to Kansas City where we had a half-hour layover. I was wandering around the terminal in my clerical collar, when a man approached me and asked if he could make his confession. We sat down in the relative privacy of the Delta Crown Room and he began. His life had been scarred with serious sin. Midway through, he started to cry. Embracing him I found myself in tears, reassuring him of the joy in the kingdom over the return of a repentant sinner and reminding him that the Prodigal Son experienced an intimacy with his father that his sinless, self-righteous brother never knew.

The man's face was transfigured. The merciful love of the redeeming God broke through his guilt and self-hatred. I prayed a prayer of thanksgiving for the Lord's unbearable forgiveness, infinite patience, and tender love. The man wept for joy. As we parted, he glowed with the radiance of a saved sinner.

As I fastened my seatbelt in the DC-10, I heard an inner voice like a bell clanging deep in my soul: *Brennan, would you do for yourself what you have just done for your brother? Would you so eagerly and enthusiastically forgive yourself, accept yourself, and love yourself?* Then words that I had heard Francis MacNutt speak at a gathering in Atlantic City, New Jersey, pierced my heart: "If the Lord Jesus Christ has washed you in his own blood and forgiven you all your sins, how dare you refuse to forgive yourself?"

Self-hatred is an indecent luxury that no disciple can afford. Self-hatred subtly reestablishes me as the center of my focus and concern. Biblically, that is idolatry. Gentleness toward myself issues in gentleness with others. It is also the precondition for my approach to God in prayer. Small wonder that the late Paul Tillich defined faith as "the courage to accept acceptance."

A life of love lived unpretentiously for others flowing out of a life lived for God is the imitation of Christ and the only authentic discipleship. A life of service through unglamorous, unpublicized works of mercy is a life marked by the signature of Jesus.

In *The Scent of Love,* Keith Miller writes that the early Church grew "not because of the [spiritual gifts] of Christians—such as the gift of speaking in tongues—and not because Christianity was such a palatable doctrine (to the contrary, it is about the most unpalatable doctrine there is) but because they had discovered the secret of community":

Generally they did not have to lift a finger to evangelize. Someone would be walking down a back alley in Corinth or Ephesus and would see a group of people sitting together talking about the strangest things—something about a man and a tree and an execution and an empty tomb. What they were talking about made no sense to the onlooker. But there was something about the way they spoke to one another, about the way they looked at one another, about the way they cried together, the way they laughed together, the way they touched one another that was strangely appealing. It gave off the scent of love. The onlooker would start to drift farther down the alley, only to be pulled back to this little group like a bee to a flower. He would listen some more, still not understanding, and start to drift away again. But again he would be pulled back, thinking, I don't have the slightest idea what these people are talking about, but whatever it is, I want part of it.[5]

The third feature of Jesus' life and teaching crucial for discipleship in the world today is *simplicity of life*. When Jesus tells us not to lay up treasure for ourselves on earth, it is because he knows that where our treasure is, our heart is. And the heart of a disciple belongs to no one but God. A Christian admits no dependence on anything else. His only master is the Lord Jesus Christ.

Secular life is concerned frantically with escape from the fear of death—through novelty, variety, physical beauty, and possessions. John Silber, president of Boston University, blasts the self-centered hedonism of our culture: "The gospel preached during every television show is 'You only go around once in life, so get all the gusto you can.' It is a statement about theology; it is a statement about beer. It's lousy beer and even worse theology."[6]

The teaching of Jesus on the uncluttered life and his injunction to travel light are well known: "Do not take along any gold or silver or copper in your belts; take no bag for the journey, or extra tunic, or sandals or a staff" (Matthew 10:9–10). Do not worry "about your life, what you will eat; or about your body, what you will wear" (Luke 12:22). In the same chapter Jesus depicts a man who is busy building bigger barns and calls him a fool. All these sayings are cautions, loving encouragement from Jesus not to get distracted, waylaid, and ambushed by stuff that moth and rust consume and that has no enduring value. A Christian's simplicity of life is striking proof that he has found what he seeks, that he has stumbled onto the treasure hidden in the field.

This is one dimension of simplicity that Jesus proposes boldly and frequently for would-be disciples. Another dimension is its contrast with complexity. A favorite slogan in Alcoholics Anonymous is the acronym K.I.S.S.—Keep It Simple, Stupid—meaning don't complicate this simple but demanding program for sobriety.

Our lives in the global village have grown overly complex and overly crowded. New obligations grow overnight like Jack's beanstalk. Our days become a never-ending succession of appointments, committee meetings, burdens, and responsibilities. We are too busy to smell the flowers, to waste time with our spouses, to befriend our children, to cultivate true friends, or to be friends to those who have no friends. Our children's schools demand our time. The civic problems of our community need our attention. Our professional status, our playtime, our membership in various organizations stake their claims. We run around, like Lancelot's horse, in four directions at once.

Weary and breathless, we sense that life is slipping away. We change our wardrobe, slip into the costume for the next performance, and regret that we have tasted so little of the peace and joy that Jesus promised. What of prayer, silence, solitude, and simple presence of the indwelling God? *Well, I'll get around to it, but not today. This week is just too full.*

The fallacy here is blaming the complexity of our lives on the complexity of our environment. How many people have told me they would love to live on some remote South Sea island or get back to the good old horse-and-buggy days when Sunday was spent visiting Grandma and Grandpa on the farm? It doesn't work because we bring our feverish, unintegrated selves to these remote places. Simplicity of life does not depend upon simplicity of environment.

The real problem lies within. Outer distractions reflect a lack of inner integration. "We are trying to be several selves at once. There is the civic self, the parental self, the financial self, the spiritual self, the society self, the professional self. And yet we are uneasy, strained, and fearful that we are shallow."[7] Driving along the turnpike or sitting in front of the TV, there comes a whispered call to the abundant life we have been neglecting: *Come to the water and slake your thirst*. It is a hint that there is a way of life more satisfying than our hurried pace. We all know people who seem to have mastered the pressures and stress of life, who don't feel guilty about saying no—in fact they say it with the same confidence as yes. They are no moony-eyed mystics but busy people carrying the same full load we are, but unhurried, unworried, with a gleam in their eye and a spring in their step. While we are tense and uptight, they are poised and at peace.

If following Jesus has anything to say to us in the real world in which we live, it speaks to us right here. Our life in Christ is meant to be lived out of the Center. Lodged within us is the power to live a life of peace, integration, and confidence. The sole requirement for tapping it is intensity of desire. If you really want to live out of the Center, you will. We have all heard the gentle whisper of the Spirit in our lives. At times we have followed the whisper, and the result was amazing equilibrium of life, joy, energy, and clarity of mind. Our outward life became simplified on the basis of inner integration.

Dominique Voillaume yielded to the Center and his life became simple. It had singleness of vision: "All that is not the love of God has no meaning for me." Much of our activity seems important to us. The six o'clock news is a command performance. An hour at the vanity table is like an audience with the Pope. We can't say no because these events seem indispensable. But if we "center down" and take our daily agenda into the silent places of the heart with honesty, openness, and willingness, much of our activity loses its importance and inviolability.

For a moment let me speak intimately about Jesus, whose love is dearer than life itself. Do you really want to live your life in his presence? Do you long for him?

Let us suppose it were so ordained that your eternal destiny was to depend on your personal relationship with a spiritual leader you know. Would you not arrange to spend a little more time with that person than you presently do? Wouldn't you strive to prove worthy of his friendship? Wouldn't you try assiduously to eliminate all personality traits displeasing to him from your life? When duties and obligations called you away from his presence, wouldn't you be eager to return to him as "the deer pants for streams of water"?

And if this person confided to you that he kept a diary of personal memoirs that were the deepest whisperings of his inner self, wouldn't you be anxious not only to read them but to steep yourself in them so that you might know and love him more?

There are certain questions that every Christian must answer in utter candor. Do you hunger for Jesus Christ? Do you yearn to spend time alone with him in prayer? Is he the most important person in your life? Does he fill your soul like a song of joy? Is he on your lips as a shout of praise? Do you eagerly turn to his memoirs, his Testament, to learn more of him? Are you making the effort to die daily to anything and everything that inhibits, threatens, or diminishes your friendship?

To discern where you really are with the Lord, recall

what saddened you in the past week. Was it the realization that you don't love Jesus enough? That you neglected opportunities to show compassion for another? Or did you get depressed over lack of recognition, criticism from an authority figure, finances, lack of friends, fears about the future, your bulging waistline?

Conversely, what gladdened you the past week? The joy of slowly praying, "Abba, Father"? The afternoon you stole away for an hour, with the Scriptures as your only companion? A small victory over selfishness? Or were the sources of your joy a new car, a new suit, a movie and a pizza, a trip to Paris or Peoria? Are you worshipping idols?

When disciples surrender to the mystery of the fire of the Spirit that burns within; when we submit to the truth that we reach life only through death; when we acknowledge that the grain of wheat must vanish into the ground, that Jonah must be buried in the belly of the whale, that the alabaster jar of self must be broken if others are to perceive the sweet fragrance of Christ; when we respond to the call of Jesus, which is not "Come to a prayer meeting" but "Come to *me*," then the limitless power of the Holy Spirit will be unleashed with astonishing force. The discipline of the secret will be a compelling sign to the church and the culture. The term *charismatic renewal* will fall into disuse. The body of Christ will be plunged into a *revolution*.

Clearly, discipleship is a revolutionary way of living. A life lived in simplicity for God and others is what Paul had in mind when he wrote in Ephesians 4:23–24, "Be renewed in the spirit of your mind, and put on the new self, which in the likeness of God has been created in righteousness and holiness of the truth" (NASB).

Personally, I take great comfort in the life stories of the first disciples. Their response was flawed by fear and hesitation. What they shared in common was dullness, an embarrassing inability to understand what Jesus was all about. Their track record was not good: They complained, they misunderstood, they quarreled, they wavered, they deserted, they denied. But Christ's reaction to their broken, inconsistent discipleship was one of unending love.

The good news is that Jesus Christ is the same yesterday, today, and forever.

Chapter Six

PASCHAL
SPIRITUALITY

*I*N WILLIAM BAUSCH's splendid book *Storytelling,
Imagination, and Faith*, he recounts the following story:

> An old Mississippi country preacher believed in his
> bones that the Word of God is a two-edged sword.
> One Sunday morning he mounted the pulpit and
> prayed: "Oh, Lord, give thy servant this mornin' the
> eyes of the eagle and the wisdom of the owl; con-
> nect his soul with the gospel telephone in the cen-
> tral skies; illuminate his brow with the Sun of
> Heaven; possess his mind with love for the people;
> turpentine his imagination; grease his lips with

possum oil; electrify his brain with the lightnin' of the Word; put perpetual motion in his arms; fill him plumb full of dynamite of Thy glory; anoint him all over with the kerosene of salvation, and set him on fire. Amen!"[1]

Amen, indeed!

Jesus did not come to bring peace but the sword, not nightgowns but the armor of God. The kingdom of God is not a matter of words but of power, a source of transformation and information. The spiritual life is simply life itself lived with the vision of faith. Any spirituality claiming the name *Christian* must resonate with the life and teaching of the Master.

The New Testament writings establish the essential characteristics of the early church. What is central in the New Testament should be central in the life of the church today. Whatever is fringe or peripheral in the New Testament should not be made central today. (Thus, for example, any preoccupation with the gift of tongues is according undue weight to a marginal matter.)

Jesus Christ, in the mystery of his death and resurrection, is the center of the New Testament, from Matthew's genealogy to Revelation's "Maranatha." His breakthrough from death to life—*pesach* in Hebrew, Pasch in English—is the core of the gospel proclamation and the entire Christian faith. Therefore, it can be unequivocally stated: To understand the paschal mystery of Easter is to understand Christianity; to be ignorant of the paschal mystery is to be ignorant of Christianity.

There is one spirituality in the church of the Lord Jesus: *paschal spirituality*. Essentially, it is our daily death to sin, selfishness, dishonesty, and degraded love in order to rise to newness of life. Paul says, "It is no longer I who live, but Christ lives in me" (Galatians 2:20, NASB). Each time we deal a mortal blow to the ego, the pasch of Jesus is traced in our flesh. Each time we choose to walk the extra mile, to turn the other cheek, to embrace and not reject, to be compassionate and not competitive, to kiss and not bite, to forgive and not massage the latest bruise to our wounded ego, we are breaking through from death to life.

The biblical word for conversion is *metanoia*, meaning a radical transformation of our inner self. We discover that a personal relationship with Jesus Christ no longer can be contained in a code of do's and don'ts. It becomes, as Jeremiah wrote, a covenant written in the fleshy tablets of the heart and inscribed in the depths of our being. Conversion opens us to a new agenda, new priorities, a different hierarchy of values. It stretches us from professing Jesus as Savior to confessing him as Lord, from a mindless accommodation of our faith in our culture to a lived faith in the consuming truth of the gospel. It turpentines our imagination, electrifies our brain with the lightnin' of the Word, fills us plumb full of the dynamite of his glory, and anoints us all over with the kerosene of salvation and sets us on fire!

The opposite of conversion is aversion. The other side of metanoia is paranoia. Paranoia is usually understood in psychological terms. It is characterized by fear, suspicion, and flight from reality. Paranoia usually results in elaborate illusions and self-deception. In the biblical context paranoia implies more than emotional or mental imbalance. It refers to an attitude of being, a stance of the heart. Spiritual paranoia is a flight from God and from our true selves. It is an attempt to escape from personal responsibility. It is the tendency to avoid the cost of discipleship and to seek out an escape route from the demands of the gospel. Paranoia of the spirit is an attempt to deny the reality of Jesus in such a way that we rationalize our behavior and choose our own way.[2]

Each of us lives in the tension between metanoia and paranoia. We walk the narrow ridge between fidelity and betrayal. None of us is immune to the seduction of counterfeit discipleship. A watered-down gospel would allow us to have the best of both worlds, a life of gilded mediocrity wherein we carefully distribute ourselves between flesh and spirit with a watchful eye on both. The gospel of cheap grace dilutes faith into a lukewarm mix of Bible, nationalism, and compromise—a spirituality that bears no resemblance to the paschal mystery of the death and resurrection of Jesus.

What are the characteristics of paschal spirituality? There are seven of them.

First, a paschal spirituality is Christocentric, meaning it is through Christ, with Christ, and in Christ. This may seem so self-evident that it hardly merits our attention. But Christian history, both past and present, is the ongoing story of a tragic distortion of faith when Jesus Christ ceases to be the center of the Christian life. In the past, certain devotional practices have received so much attention in thought and teaching that direct devotion to the person of Jesus Christ in and through the church has taken second place. In other Christian circles, the tendency to "absolutize" certain sections of the New Testament (for instance, Acts 1–3 and 1 Corinthians 12–14) has placed an emphasis on peak religious experiences and spectacular gifts of the Spirit—with the result that the mystery of the death and resurrection has been relegated to the margins of Christian faith and practice.

In recent years, preoccupation with styles of worship—traditional or renewed, organ or guitar, hymns or choruses, incense or balloons, recited or spontaneous prayers, old or new translations of the Bible—have upstaged the central drama of Calvary and Easter morning. Style overshadows substance, form transcends content, the church supplants Jesus. As we noted earlier, a Christian's right thinking is the new standard for determining what he or she is or is not worth in the sight of God and everyone else.

Above the din the Father cries out, "You go to church every Sunday and read your Bible, but the body of my Son is broken! You memorize chapter and verse and honor all your traditions, but the body of my Son is broken! You recite the creed and defend orthodoxy, but the body of my Son is broken! You hark back to tradition and press forward toward renewal, but the body of my Son is broken!"

At this point in church history I believe it is imperative to remember that the Christ of John's Gospel asked Peter (who had denied him three times) only one question: "Do you love me?" The criterion by which Christ measures his friends and repudiators is still "Do you love me?" What is the good of Bible study, reform, and renewal if we forget this, even if we hold to everything else? How can anyone muster the incredible hardheartedness and the intemperate messianic zeal to inflate style and tradition, orthodoxy, biblical interpretation, and right thinking into such monsters that Jesus' question to Peter and us is put on the shelf?

The author of the fourth Gospel puts but one question to his readers: Do we *know* Jesus? To know him is life. Everything else fades into twilight and darkness. For the evangelist John, what constitutes dignity in the Christian community is not apostleship or office, not titles, not the gifts of prophecy or healing or inspired preaching, but only intimacy with Jesus. This is a status that all Christians enjoy.

To our contemporary church, which treats chief administrative officials and charismatic superstars with excessive deference, the Gospel of John sends this prophetic word: The love of Jesus Christ alone gives status in the Christian community. In his powerful pastoral book *The Churches the Apostles Left Behind*, Raymond Brown writes:

> All Christians are disciples and among them greatness is determined by a loving relationship with Jesus, not by function or office. Church offices and even apostleship are of lesser importance when

compared to discipleship, which is literally a question of eternal life or death. Within that discipleship, there are no second-class Christians.[3]

The thrust of paschal spirituality is Christocentric. It never loses sight of Christ's question, "Do you love me?" nor does it try to go the Master one better. Even if everything is in confusion, nothing is finally ruined as long as disciples will still follow him, be held fast by him, learn from him, and love him.

A few years ago, a white prisoner died of a heart attack in a Montgomery, Alabama, jail. While in prison he had had a profound conversion experience and entered into an authentic relationship with Jesus. The convict in the next cell, a huge black man, was a cynic. Each night the white prisoner spoke through the prison bars and told his fellow prisoner about the love of Jesus. The black man mocked him, told him he was sick in the head, that religion was the last refuge of the insane. Nonetheless, the white prisoner passed Scripture passages to him and shared his candy whenever he received a gift from a relative. At the white man's funeral service, when the prison chaplain spoke of the Easter victory of Jesus, the burly black prisoner stood up in the middle of the sermon, pointed to the coffin, and said, "That's the only Jesus I ever knew."

Paschal spirituality says that if our Christian journey does not produce Christ in us, if the passing years do not form Jesus in us in such a way that we really resemble him, our spirituality is bankrupt.

A second characteristic of paschal spirituality is that it is aware of the community of God's people. We belong to God's people. Christianity can never be an affair that simply embraces our individual happiness. Paschal spirituality avoids any exaggerated form of Christian individualism—a "Jesus and me" mentality. God did not call us into salvation in isolation but in community. Our personal destiny is but part of his magnificent saving plan that includes in its sweep not only the entire human community but the whole of creation, the inauguration of the new heavens and the new earth.

The Jesus-and-me mindset tells us that all we have to do is accept Christ as Savior, read the Bible, go to church, and save our souls. Christianity becomes simply a telephone booth affair, a private conversation between God and me without reference to my brothers and sisters. I go to church on Sunday while the world goes to hell. When preoccupation with my personal salvation drugs me into such insensitivity that I no longer hear the bleating of the lost sheep, then Karl Marx was right: Religion is the opiate of the people.

For the Christian, one dislocating, self-impoverishing hour spent with a child living in a broken-down dump is worth more than all the burial mounds of rhetoric, all the enfeebled good intentions, all the mumbling and fumbling and tardiness of those Christians who are so busy cultivating their own holiness that they cannot hear the anguished cry of the child in the slum.

The Christian life is meant to be lived in community. And community life is a radical imitation of the holy and undivided Trinity who is dialogue, spontaneous love, and relationship. "No one has ever seen God; but if we love one another, God lives in us and his love is made complete in us" (1 John 4:12). Paschal spirituality insists that to love one another means the love of God has reached full growth in our lives.

> A Gentile once came to Rabbi Shammai and said, "Convert me to Judaism on the condition that you can teach me the whole Torah while I am standing on one foot." With a rod in his hand Rabbi Shammai angrily threw him out. Then the man went to Rabbi Hillel and repeated his request. "Convert me to Judaism on the condition that you can teach me the whole Torah while I am standing on one foot." Rabbi Hillel converted him and taught him as follows: "What is hateful to you, do not do to your neighbor." This is the whole Torah. All the rest is commentary.[4]

Paul says that he who loves his neighbor has fulfilled the entire law and the prophets (see Romans 13:10). The words of Charles de Foucauld, "One learns to love God by loving men and women," surge from the very heart of the Christian tradition. This is the mind of Christ.

> We love because he first loved us. If anyone says, "I love God," yet hates his brother, he is a liar. For anyone who does not love his brother, whom he has seen, cannot love God, whom he has not seen. And he has given us this command: Whoever loves God must also love his brother. (1 John 4:19–21)

Paschal spirituality says that the truest test of discipleship is the way we live with each other in the community of faith. It is as simple and as demanding as that. In our words and deeds we give shape and form to our faith every day. We make people a little better or leave them a little worse. We either affirm or deprive, enlarge or diminish the lives of others.

> The kingdom, Jesus tells us, is in our very midst, in the mystery of our relationships with each other. We are within its gates when we draw close to one another with the love that is fired by the Spirit. We are already on sacred ground when we reach out to understand rather than condemn, when we forgive rather than seek revenge, when as unarmed pilgrims we are ready to meet our enemies. What Jesus teaches is too simple and too wonderful for those who want magic in their religion.[5]

According to the evangelical criterion for holiness, the person closest to the heart of Jesus Christ is not the one who prays the most, studies Scripture the most, or the one who has the most important position of spiritual responsibility entrusted to his or her care. It is the one who loves the most, and that is not my opinion. It is the Word who will judge us.

A third characteristic of paschal spirituality: It looks upon human nature as fallen but redeemed—flawed but, in essence, good. The emotions are good, needing only direction and grace, not suppression. We are Christians, not Stoics. We could do with a good deal less of the pessimism found in some Christian circles regarding earthy things. Creation is the overflow of the goodness of God and his infinite love. In response to the question "Why did God make the world?" paschal spirituality replies that God the Father had this thing about *being*. As Robert Capon put it (in a quotation for which I long ago lost the source):

> He was absolutely wild about being. He kept thinking up new ways of being and new kinds of being to be. One afternoon, God the Son came along and said, "This is really great stuff. Why don't I go out and mix up a batch?" And God the Holy Spirit said, "Terrific! I'll help you."
>
> So they got together that night after supper and put on a tremendous show of being for the Father. It was full of water and light and frogs; pussy willows kept dropping all over the place, and speckled fish swam around in the wine glasses. There were mushrooms and grapes, horseradishes and tigers—and men and women everywhere to taste them, juggle them, join with them, and love them. God the Father looked at the whole wild party and said, "Wonderful. Just what I had in mind. Yeh!" And all God the Son and Holy Spirit could think of was to say, "Yeh, yeh!" They laughed for ages saying things like how great it was for being to be, how clever of the Father to conceive the idea, how kind of the Son to go to all the trouble to put it together, and how gracious of the Spirit to devote so much time to choreography. They told old jokes

to one another, and the Father and Son drank their wine in the unity of the Holy Spirit and threw ripe olives and pickled mushrooms at each other forever and ever.

Admittedly this is a crass analogy, but perhaps crass analogies are the safest. Everyone knows that God is not a bearded old man throwing olives. But not everyone is convinced that God is not merely a "cosmic force," an "uncaused cause," an "immovable mover," or any of the other analogies we use about him. The image of creation as the result of a hilarious Trinitarian bash might be bonkers, but it does hint at the truth that God takes delight in his creation.

Creation, Genesis says, is good. Created things are just so many myriad responses to the delight of God who wills them into being. Thomas Aquinas said being is good in itself. Being and good are interchangeable.

Of course, it is not always easy to see that all being is good. Affirming our faith in the goodness of creation becomes problematic in the face of an earthquake in Mexico City that claims five thousand lives, or the mudslide in Colombia that kills forty thousand. In addition, as Capon notes, there are poison toadstools, cancer cells, liver flukes, killer whales, and loan sharks to be considered. But there is no retreating from the revelation in the Word: "God saw all that he had made, and it was very good" (Genesis 1:31).

Human nature, freed from the slavery of sin, is capable of awesome holiness. Evangelist Robert Frost, in an address in San Jose, California, remarked, "The Lord brought me up short with the challenge: 'Why do you persist in seeing your children in the hands of the devil, rather than in the arms of their faithful Shepherd?' I then realized that in my mind I had been imagining the evils of the present age as being more powerful than the timeless love of God."

Paschal spirituality recovers the element of delight in creation. Imagine the ecstasy, the cry of joy when God makes a person in his own image! When God made you! The Father gives you as a gift to himself. You are a response to the vast delight of God. Out of an infinite number of possibilities, God invested you and me with existence.

In light of the truth, I have to ask myself, *Have I really appreciated the wondrous gift that I am? Or do I measure my worth by the texture of my hair, the structure of my face, or the size of my waist-line?* Could the Father's gift to himself be anything but beautiful? I sing of his other gifts—"girls in white dresses with blue satin sashes, snowflakes that stay on my nose and eyelashes."[6] Why don't I like my beautiful self? Paschal spirituality says that because of the death and resurrection of Jesus Christ I can love myself not in spite of my flaws and warts but with them. Such is the acceptance of the God of Jesus.

Fourth, paschal spirituality is stamped with the signature of Jesus. There is no genuine Christianity where the sign of the Cross is absent. Cheap grace is grace without the Cross, an intellectual assent to a dusty pawnshop of doctrinal beliefs while drifting aimlessly with the cultural values of the secular city. Discipleship without sacrifice breeds a comfortable Christianity barely distinguishable in its mediocrity from the rest of the world. The Cross is both the test and the destiny of a follower of Christ.

> What we desperately need to reunderstand is that it is dangerous to be a true Christian. Anyone who takes his or her Christianity seriously will realize that crucifixion is not something that happened to one man nineteen hundred and fifty-odd years ago, nor was martyrdom just the fate of his early followers. It should be an omnipresent risk for every Christian. Christians should—need—in certain ways to live dangerously if they are to live out their faith. The times have made this apparent. Today the times demand of us that we take major risks for peace. And in combating the entrenched forces of the arms race—the principalities and powers of this world—that very much includes the risk of martyrdom.... It is time for communal, congregational action and corporate risk.[7]

Tepid preaching and lifeless worship have spread so many ashes on the fire of the gospel that we scarcely feel the glow anymore. We have gotten so used to the ultimate Christian fact—Jesus naked, stripped, crucified, and risen—that we no longer see it for what it is: a summons to strip ourselves of earthly cares and worldly wisdom, of all desire for human praise, of greediness for any kind of comfort (spiritual consolations included). It is a summons to readiness to stand up and be counted as peacemakers in a violent world. It is a call to let go of the pretense that we really aren't worldly (the kind of worldliness that prefers the more attractive duty to the less attractive and leads us to put out more effort for people we want to stand well with). Even the last rag we cling to—the self-flattery that suggests we are being humble when we disclaim any resemblance to Jesus Christ—even that rag has to go when we stand face-to-face with the crucified Son of God.

Charles Colson, Watergate crook and wheeler-dealer par excellence, is a witness to many aspects of resurrection-centered spirituality. His awareness of salvation-in-community speaks for itself through his prison ministry. In addition, his life is a lovely letter to God signed with the signature of Jesus. Recently he learned that he has a malignant cancer. He thought he would be shattered, but he discovered in his confrontation with fear and suffering that there is nothing for which God does not pour out His grace abundantly. The tumor was caught early, and doctors have assured him that the prognosis is excellent.

Colson said, "My suffering provided some fresh insights...into the health-and-wealth gospel. If God really delivers his people from all pain and illness, as is so often claimed, why was I so sick? Had my faith become weak? Had I fallen from favor? No, I had always recognized such teaching as false theology. But after four weeks in a maximum care unit, I came to see it as something else: a presumptuous stumbling block to real evangelism."

Dragging his I.V. pole down a hospital corridor, Colson was asked by a Hindu visiting his desperately ill son whether or not God would heal the boy if he, the father, were to be born again. "He said he had heard things like that on television. As I listened, I realized how arrogant health-and-wealth religion sounds to suffering families. Christians can be spared suffering, but little Hindu children go blind. One couldn't blame a Hindu or Muslim or agnostic for resenting, even hating, such a God." As for his cancer, "We don't begin to know all the reasons why. But we do know that our suffering and weakness can be an opportunity to witness to the world the amazing grace of God at work through us."[8]

Paschal spirituality is nothing less than bondage to Jesus Christ alone, a complete attachment to his person, a sharing in the rhythm of his death and resurrection, a participation in his life of sorrow, rejection, loneliness, and suffering. To paraphrase Francis Thompson, "The wood must be charred before He can limn with it."

A fifth dimension of paschal spirituality: It is joyful and optimistic. It is anchored in hope. It eagerly looks forward to the final glorification of the Second Coming. The cry of the Christian is, "There's gonna be a great day!" The faithful God who led his children into the Promised Land will lead us into the promised land of glory where the victory of Jesus Christ will shine like a neon light in the skies and angelic trumpets will announce the final harvest. The true Christian is the lover separated from his beloved—the day of reunion cannot come too soon. Such is the happy, hopeful, buoyant spirit that characterizes paschal spirituality. It should set the tone of our life in Christ, day by day.

Here is the root and source of Christian joy, mirth, and laughter. It is why theologian Robert Hotchkins can insist, "Christians ought to be celebrating constantly":

We ought to be preoccupied with parties, banquets, feasts, and merriment. We ought to give ourselves over to veritable orgies of joy because of our belief in resurrection. We ought to attract people to our faith quite literally by the fun there is in being a Christian. Unfortunately, however, we too readily become somber, serious, and pompous. We fly in the face of our own tradition because we are afraid of wasting time or getting attached. In the words of Teresa of Avila, "from silly devotions and sour-faced saints, spare us, O Lord."

The victory of Jesus Christ at Calvary presents us with only two logical alternatives: Either you believe in the resurrection, and hence you believe in Jesus of Nazareth and the gospel he preached; or you believe in nonresurrection and do not believe in Jesus of Nazareth and the gospel he preached. If Easter is not history, we must become cynics. In other words, either we believe in resurrection and a living Jesus who is with us in faith, and we commit our lives to both, or we do not. Either we dismiss the Good News as too good to be true, or we permit ourselves to be overwhelmingly joyful persons because of it. A Christian is called to believe in a God who loves and in his Christ who is risen. We believe, and we believe strongly; we believe, and we believe joyously.

Joy in the risen Jesus is directly connected with the quality of our faith. Mother Teresa chose to live her life among the most afflicted of God's children, yet she could say, "Never let anything so fill your heart with grief that you forget the joy of the risen Lord."

Ignatius of Loyola encouraged Christians to pray often for intense gladness.[9] He wasn't talking about a giddy, cocktail-party gaiety or a brave attempt to smile through the tears. This is a deep-seated gladness rooted in the victory and promise of the risen Jesus. Compassion, the ability to suffer with the hurt of another, is an essential Christian quality; equally important is the capacity to rejoice in the happiness of another. Intense gladness is anchored in the joy that Christ now experiences at the right hand of his Father. Every tear has been wiped away. There is no more mourning or sadness in the life of the risen Jesus.

When this gift of intense gladness is given, it produces a joy that is solid and impregnable, rooted deep beneath the shifting sands of our fickle feelings. Whatever happens, the Lord is risen! Nothing can suffocate this joy and hope. Whether the day is stormy or fair, whether I am sick or in good health, nothing alters the fact that Christ is risen. In the early church, each Sunday was known as the feast of "little Easter." In our own culture the Christian Sabbath is a summons to the joy and optimism of resurrection Sunday.

The sixth aspect of paschal spirituality: It promotes unity without uniformity. Jesus is the Way, and his light is refracted in myriad ways by different personalities. He incarnates himself in new and surprising ways in each of us. Each of us is called to be a unique and singular manifestation of Christ's truth and love, not a carbon copy of someone else. We need not attempt to cast people into a certain mold, but rather be ready to recognize the rich variety of persons and personalities who blend together to make up the church. No effort is made to destroy the wealth of variety in a drive for sameness. In terms of church worship, the operative principle is unity in praising God without uniformity in style.

Finally, paschal spirituality regards persons as free. We are a free people by virtue of the freedom with which Christ has made us free. "It is for freedom that Christ has set us free" (Galatians 5:1). Christians are to be treated by religious authorities as free men and women, not slaves. We are responsible human beings with the ability to make rational decisions. Enlightened (not blind) obedience is the paschal ideal. There is ready acceptance of the truth that each person's destiny lies in his or her own hands, guided and strengthened by the grace of Christ. There is profound awareness that the fundamental secret of Jesus was his sovereign respect for human liberty. He never tried to make people virtuous against their will. This is the essential betrayal.

The institutional church is untrue to the law of its own "being" whenever it violates freedom. Whenever any authority figure seeks to suppress freedom, he or she is thereby setting himself (however unconsciously) in opposition to Christ and his church. God created us in his own image because he wanted free, responsible service. When the virtue of obedience is reduced to a pattern of domination and submission, we produce trained cowards rather than Christian persons.

Perhaps this is the hardest lesson of resurrection-centered spirituality: to look upon ourselves and others as free, responsible persons. Instead of creating more freedom, all of us unwittingly erect impediments to it—impediments such as neurotic fear, pressure, threats of punishment. The tragedy of our attempts to compel others to be virtuous by force or subtle manipulation is that these efforts are so prevalent in our lives, so characteristic of our relationships with others that most of us, most of the time, are unaware of the problem. We do not perceive that we betray a basic lack of respect for the humanity of those with whom we deal, and that this lack of respect is the essential problem with the use of authority in the church and in the home.

If we really knew the God of Jesus, we would stop trying to control and manipulate others "for their own good," knowing full well that this is not how God works among his people. Paul writes, "Where the Spirit of the Lord is, there is freedom" (2 Corinthians 3:17).

These are the central features and dominant characteristics of paschal spirituality centered in the life, death, and resurrection of Jesus Christ. Death and resurrection are not one-time events that occur only at the end of our journey. They are the pattern of our lives day after day.

> Each time we let go of the past to embrace the future we relive the paschal journey of Jesus in our flesh. Each time we allow our fears or selfishness to die, we break through to new life. Each time we open ourselves to the Spirit so that he can break down the walls of suspicion and bitterness, we come home to ourselves, the community, and the Lord. "I die daily," Paul wrote. He might have added, "And daily I am raised up to new life."[10]

To write the letter of our lives above the signature of Jesus is to recognize his dying and rising as they are traced in our actions and carved in our hearts. In such a context, death will not be a new experience for us, nor will resurrection!

Chapter Seven

CELEBRATE
the DARKNESS

A CERTAIN CHRISTIAN thought it was of vital importance to be poor and austere. It had never dawned on him that the vitally important thing was to drop his ego, that the ego fattens on holiness just as much as on worldliness, on poverty as on riches, on austerity as on luxury. There is nothing the ego will not seize upon to inflate itself.

DISCIPLE: "I have come to you with nothing in my hands."
MASTER: "Then drop it at once!"
DISCIPLE: "But how can I drop it? It is nothing."
MASTER: "Then carry it around with you! You can make a possession of your nothing. And carry your renunciation

around you like a trophy. Don't drop your possessions. Drop your ego."[1]

Death to self is necessary in order to live for God. A crucifixion of the ego is required. That is why mature Christian prayer inevitably leads to the purification of what St. John of the Cross called the dark night of the senses and the spirit which, through loneliness and aridity, buries egoism and leads us out of ourselves to experience God.

The "dark night" is a very real place, as anyone who has been there will tell you. Alan Jones calls it "the second conversion." While the first conversion was characterized by joy and enthusiasm and filled with felt consolation and a profound sense of God's presence, the second is marked by dryness, barrenness, desolation, and a profound sense of God's *absence*. The dark night is an indispensable stage of spiritual growth both for the individual Christian and the church.

Merton writes:

> There is an absolute need for the solitary, bare, dark, beyond-thought, beyond-feeling type of prayer.... Unless that dimension is there in the church somewhere, the whole caboodle lacks life and light and intelligence. It is a kind of hidden, secret, unknown stabilizer and compass too. About this I have no hesitation or doubts.[2]

Though painful, the purification of the ego in the dark night is the high road to Christian freedom and maturity. In fact, it is often an answer to prayer.

Have you ever prayed that you might be more prayerful? Have you ever prayed for a lively and conscious awareness of God's indwelling presence throughout the day? Have you ever prayed that you might be gentle and humble in heart? Have you ever asked for a spirit of detachment from material things, personal relationships, and creature comforts? Have you ever cried out for an increase in faith?

I know I have, and I suspect that we have all prayed often for these spiritual gifts. But I wonder if we really meant what we said when we asked for these things? Did we really want what we asked for? I think not. Otherwise, why did we recoil in shock and sorrow when our prayers were answered? The suffering involved in arriving at the answer made us sorry we ever asked in the first place.

We ask for spiritual growth and Christian maturity, but we really don't want them—at least not in the way God chooses to grant them. For example, if we ask the Lord to make us more prayerful, how does he answer our prayer? By bringing us to our knees in adversity and suffering. Have you ever heard a Christian complain, "What happened? The week after I was 'born again,' all hell broke loose. I lost my job and my car keys, quarreled with my wife, got on the wrong plane, and wound up in Philadelphia instead of San Francisco."

Through a sequence of human events (divinely inspired), the God and Father of our Lord Jesus Christ leads us into a state of interior devastation. When we are like this, it is highly probable (though not inevitable) that we become more prayerful. Up to now perhaps we had not been praying in depth. But now we are truly praying. We might not be saying all that many prayers, and we might not be following the set formulas that we presumed were prayer, but we are praying as never before. God is drawing us closer to himself. We ask, "What's happening?" And the answer comes: "Don't you remember? This is what you asked for. There is no cheap grace. You wanted to be more prayerful. Now you are."

Our original petition was to achieve a constant state of prayerfulness. Well, nothing inspires prayer like adversity, sorrow, and humiliation. In these broken times we pray at our best. Our prayer rises in simplicity: "Lord Jesus Christ, Son of God, I trust in you." Or, "Abba, I belong to you." In Catherine de Hueck Doherty's words, "We put our head into our heart and our cerebral short-sightedness is cured."

When we pray for the gift of a prayerful heart, the Lord strips away props we might lean on and leads us into spiritual desolation, into the dark night of the soul, in order that we might pray with a pure heart. As the second-century Shepherd of Hermas said, "Let us be careful not to seek mystical experiences when we should be seeking repentance and conversion." That is the beginning of our cry to God: "Lord, make me what I should be; change me, whatever the cost." And when we have said these dangerous words, we should be prepared for God to hear them. These words are dangerous because God's love is remorseless. God wants our salvation with the determination due its importance. And, the Shepherd of Hermas concludes, "God does not leave us until he has broken our hearts and our bones."[3]

Jesus says, "Learn from me, for I am gentle and humble in heart" (Matthew 11:29). These beautiful words are a portrait of the heart of Christ. So we respond, "Jesus, gentle and humble in heart, make my heart like yours." Now we are really in for it! We have just opened Pandora's box. Why? Because we don't learn humility by reading about it in spiritual books or listening to its praises in sermons. We learn humility directly from the Lord Jesus in whatever way he wishes to teach us. Most often we learn humility through humiliations.

What is humility? It is the stark realization and acceptance of the fact that I am totally dependent upon God's love and mercy. It grows through a stripping away of all self-sufficiency. Humility is not caught by repeating pious phrases; it is accomplished by the hand of God. It is Job on the dunghill all over again as God reminds us that *he* is our only true hope.

I know a man who felt comfortably close to Christ for thirty years because his ministry had been a success. He had made his mark, produced good work, and was respected and esteemed by the community. It appeared as though his success was the reward for his faithfulness. Then one day God took pity on him and granted his prayer to be humble in heart.

What happened?

In a blinding moment of truth, the man saw his ministerial success as riddled with vanity and self-seeking. Soon friends drifted away. His popularity waned. He became conscious of distrust on the parts of others. Radical differences developed over issues such as church growth and evangelism. Sickness brought inactivity and heightened the sense of loss.

The man entered the dark night. For the first time he experienced the unbearable absence of God in his life. He suspected that his life had been a disappointment to God, a disappointment he was powerless to undo. He felt he had lost Jesus through pride and selfishness. He was convinced that the rebuke of the divine Judge in the book of Revelation was aimed at him: "You say, 'I am rich; I have acquired wealth and do not need a thing.' But you do not realize that you are wretched, pitiful, poor, blind and naked" (3:17).

The pain was excruciating, the dark night pitch-black. Later, however, when the man looked back on that painful experience of ego-reduction, he recognized his agony was an answer to prayer, that the humiliation he endured was God's way of saying yes to his plea to be more like Jesus.

Biblically, there is nothing more detestable than a self-sufficient person. He is so full of himself, so swollen with pride and conceit that he is insufferable. Here is a scenario that plays in my mind.

A humble woman seeks me out because of my renown as a spiritual guide. She is simple and direct: "Please teach me how to pray."

Tersely, I inquire, "Tell me about your prayer life."

She lowers her eyes and says contritely, "There's not much to tell. I say grace before meals."

Haughtily, I reply, "You say grace before meals? Isn't that nice. Madam, I say grace upon waking and retiring and grace before reading the newspaper and turning on the television. I say grace before ambulating and defecating, before the theater and the opera, before jogging, swimming, hiking, dining, lecturing, writing. I even say grace before I say grace!"

And God whispers to me, "You ungrateful swine. Even the desire to say grace is itself my gift."

There is an ancient Christian legend that goes this way:

Where the Son of God was nailed to the cross and gave up his spirit, he went straight down to hell from the cross and set free all the sinners who were there in torment. And the devil wept and mourned for he thought he would get no more sinners for hell.

Then God said to him, "Do not weep, for I shall send you all those holy people who have become self-complacent in the consciousness of their goodness and self-righteous in their condemnation of sinners. And hell shall be filled up once more for generations until I come again."[4]

Most of the time, the self-sufficient Christian is blind to his arrogant pretensions. Even prayer is used for self-justification. He goes along his merry way reciting pious little phrases like, "Jesus, keep me humble." And at last the God who cannot be manipulated or controlled replies, "Fine. You want to be humble, do you? This sequence of humiliations and failures will take care of that."

The school of humiliation is a great learning experience; there is no other like it. When the gift of a humble heart is granted, we are more accepting of ourselves and less critical of others. Self-knowledge brings a humble and realistic awareness of our limitations. It leads us to be patient and compassionate with others, whereas before we were demanding, insensitive, and stuck-up. Gone are the complacency and narrow-mindedness that made God superfluous. For the humble person there is a constant awareness of his or her own weakness, insufficiency, and desperate need for God.

Probably the moment in my own life when I was closest to the Truth who is Jesus Christ was the experience of being a hopeless derelict in the gutter in Fort Lauderdale, Florida. In his novel *The Moviegoer,* Walker Percy writes, "Only once in my life was the grip of everydayness broken: when I lay bleeding in the ditch." Paradoxically, such an experience of powerlessness does not make one sad. It is a great relief because it makes us rely not on our own strength but on the limitless power of God. The realization that God is the main agent makes the yoke easy, the burden light, and the heart still.

Of course, the most withering experience of ego-reduction occurs when we pray, "Lord, increase my faith." We need to tread carefully here, because the life of pure faith is the dark night. In this "night" God allows us to live by faith and faith alone. Mature faith cannot grow when we are surfeited with all kinds of spiritual comforts and consolations. All these must be removed if we are to advance in the pure trust of God. The Lord withdraws all tangible supports to purify our hearts, to discern if we are in love with the gifts of the Giver or the Giver of the gifts.

The question is, do I worship God or do I worship my experience of God? Do I worship God or do I worship my idea of him? If I am to avoid a narcotic approach to religion that forces me to stagger from experience to experience hoping for bigger and better things, I must know what I believe apart from the nice or nasty feelings that may or may not accompany such a belief. The second conversion [the dark night of the soul] has to do with learning to cope and flourish when the warm feelings, consolations, and props that accompany the first conversion are withdrawn. Does faith evaporate when the initial feelings dissolve? In psychological terms, the ego has to break; and this breaking is like entering into a great darkness. Without such a struggle and affliction, there can be no movement in love.[5]

The prayer for increased faith separates the men from the boys, the women from the girls, the mystics from the romantics. In her autobiography, the thirteenth-century mystic Catherine of Siena described her prayer life as glorious. She had a highly conscious awareness of the divine indwelling. She loved to spend days alone locked up in her room enjoying the felt presence of the beautiful God who dwelt in her heart. These were times of immense spiritual consolation, mountaintop experiences, moments of intimate personal encounter. There was peace, joy, security, certitude. God, her God, was always with her. Her life in the Spirit would be an unbroken upward spiral toward holiness.

So she thought.

Until one day her comfortable life in Christ exploded. She lost the familiar feelings of the secure possession of God. The indwelling Trinity, she felt, was gone. She lost the sense of his presence and felt dead to his influence. Even the memory of him seemed unreal. God had vanished like last night's dream. Now the only thing that occupied her consciousness was sin. Impure images filled her thoughts, and her body tingled in response. She felt as though she had been plunged into a pool of filth and that she had lost forever her clean, joyous life with Christ. She was plunged into the dark night. But the darkness proved to be the matrix from which sprang light, grace, and growth in faith.

After a long period of dryness, emptiness, and aridity, without any preparation or warning, Catherine suddenly found Jesus again. She had a profound experience of his loving presence in the very room where she had been tempted so fiercely. Angrily she complained, "Lord, where were you when all those foul images tormented my mind?" The answer of Jesus led her into a new depth of faith: "Catherine, all during your temptations, I have remained with you in the depths of your heart. Otherwise, you could not have overcome them."

At that critical moment, Catherine of Siena surrendered forever her old concept of the presence of God. Jesus' words had taught her that his presence in her heart was something deeper and holier than she could imagine or feel. In this life he is always a hidden God. Human feelings cannot touch him and human thoughts cannot measure him. Personal experience cannot heighten the certainty of his presence any more than the absence of experience can lessen it. These words made Catherine realize as never before that nothing but grave, conscious, deliberate sin could separate her from the Beloved of her soul. Not noise or irritating people, distractions or temptations; not feelings of consolation or desolation, success or failure; nothing but turning back could ever separate her from the love of God made visible in Jesus Christ our Lord. He would always be there in the quiet darkness just as he promised: *Be not afraid. I will be with you.* Catherine had lost the presence of God only to find it again in the "deep and dazzling darkness" of a richer faith. The dark night was an answered prayer. She was free to celebrate the darkness.

We tend to believe that when we no longer feel the presence and consolation of God, he is no longer there. Alan Jones summarizes the theology of St. John of the Cross regarding the dark night:

> The first sign [of the dark night of the soul] is that we no longer have any pleasure or consolation either in God or in creation. Nothing pleases us. Nothing touches us. Everything and everyone seem dull and uninteresting. Life is dust and ashes in the mouth. The second sign is an abiding and biting sense of failure, even though the believer conscientiously tries to center her life on God. There is a sense of never having done enough and of needing to atone for something that has no name.
>
> The third sign, and the one that is most threatening to us today, is that it is no longer possible to

pray or meditate with the imagination. Images, pictures, and metaphors no longer seem to reach us. God (if he is there) no longer communicates with us through the senses. In more modern terms, it is a matter of living from a center other than the ego. Even to begin to do this is to enter a great darkness, a new kind of light or illumination comes; and through it our relationship to God, although more hidden than before, becomes deeper and more direct.[6]

This experience of darkness is integral to the signed lifestyle. With the ego purged and the heart purified through the trials of the dark night, the interior life of an authentic disciple is a hidden, invisible affair. Today it appears that God is calling many ordinary Christians into this rhythm of loss and gain. The hunger I encounter across the land for silence, solitude, and centering prayer is the Spirit of Christ calling us from the shallows to the deep.

Undoubtedly in each of our lives there were periods of intense fervor when we could almost touch the goodness of God. Bible studies, prayer meetings, retreats, and devotional time were precious securities to many of us. It was pleasant to think about God, a comfort to speak to him, a joy to be in his presence. Perhaps all this has changed. We may feel we have lost Christ and fear that he will never return. Now it is difficult to connect two thoughts about him. Prayer has become artificial. Words spoken to him ring hollow in our empty soul. Worse, oppressive feelings of guilt sharpen the sense of loss. Night closes in around us.

We have failed him. It is all our fault.

It is a comfort to know that this is a path that many have tracked before us. Moreover, it is reassuring to learn that the longed-for growth in faith is not far away. God's love and mercy have not abandoned us. Clouds may shroud us in darkness, but above, the sun shines bright. God's mercy never fails. The Christian who surrenders in trust to this truth finds Jesus Christ in a new way. It marks the beginning of a deeper life of faith where joy and peace flourish even in the darkness, because they are rooted, not in superficial human feelings, but deep down in the dark certainty of faith that Jesus is the same, yesterday, today, and forever.

The very inability to feel his presence with our unstable emotions, or to appreciate his goodness with our feeble thoughts, becomes a help rather than a hindrance. Joy and sorrow may play havoc with our feelings, but beneath this shifting surface God dwells in the darkness. It is there that we go to meet him; it is there that we pray in peace, silent and attentive to the God whose love knows no shadow of change. It is there that we celebrate the darkness in the quiet certainty of mature faith.

> The contemplative is not the man or woman who has fiery visions of the cherubim…but simply he who has risked his mind in the desert beyond language and beyond ideas where God is encountered in the nakedness of pure trust, that is to say, in the surrender of our poverty and incompleteness, in order no longer to clench our minds in a cramp

upon themselves, as if thinking made us exist. The message the contemplative offers is not that you need to find your way through the language and problems that today surround God, but whether you understand or not, God loves you, is present to you, lives in you, dwells in you, calls you, saves you, and offers you an understanding and light which are like nothing you have ever found in books or heard in sermons.[7]

The theology of the dark night is simplicity itself: God strips us of natural delights and spiritual consolations in order to enter more fully into our hearts. Christian maturity lies in allowing God the freedom to work his sovereign wisdom in us, neither abandoning a disciplined life of prayer in frustration nor running to the distractions the world affords us. What comes to mind is the image of a branch plunged several times into fire. As the fire scorches the wood, it burns away all the natural saps and juices proper to the wood. At first, the wood is charred and ugly. Each time it is thrust into the fire, the purging process continues. Finally, when all the natural juices that have been resisting the action of the fire are burnt away, the wood takes on the qualities of the fire itself and glows.

The graces of prayer, humility, detachment, and a deepened faith are the beautiful qualities of the flame. We can obtain those qualities only through the purging action of God's grace. In this purification process we are prepared to receive the gifts we have prayed for.

When we have hit bottom and are emptied of all we

thought important to us, then we truly pray, truly become humble and detached, and live in the bright darkness of faith. In the midst of the emptying we know that God has not deserted us. He has merely removed the obstacles keeping us from a deeper union with him. Actually we are closer to God than ever before, although we are deprived of the consolations that we once associated with our spirituality. What we thought was communion with him was really a hindrance to that communion.

Yet the dark night is not the end—only the means to union with God. We have asked God for the gift of prayer, and he visits us with adversity to bring us to our knees. We have prayed for humility, and God levels us with humiliation. We cry out for an increase of faith, and God strips us of the reassurances that we had identified with faith.

Does growth in Christ follow automatically?

No. Suffering alone does not produce a prayerful spirit. Humiliation alone does not foster humility. Desolation alone does not guarantee the increase of faith. These experiences merely dispose us to prayer, humility, and faith. We can still be wallowing in self-pity and rebellion, pride or apathy, and the last state will be worse than the first. We can eat humble pie until the bakery is bare and emerge with only tightfisted bitterness in our hands. One further crucial step in the process of ego-slaying remains.

The most characteristic feature of the humility of Jesus is his forgiveness and acceptance of others. By contrast, our nonacceptance of others and lack of forgiveness keep us in a state of agitation and unrest. Our resentments reveal that the signature of Jesus still is not written on our lives. The surest sign of union with the crucified Christ is our forgiveness of those who have perpetrated injustices against us. Without acceptance and forgiveness the dark night will be only that. The bottom line will be a troubled heart. Forgiveness of enemies seals our participation in the dark night of Jesus Christ who cried out on behalf of his killers, "Father, forgive them, for they know not what they do."

One night years ago in the monastery in Steubenville, Ohio, a number of brothers were naming the greatest book each had ever read, excluding the Bible. One learned man said *The Confessions of St. Augustine* towered over all others. Another friar nominated the *Summa Theologica* of Thomas Aquinas. A third added *The Mystalogical Catechesis* of Cyril of Jerusalem. Without blinking an eye, I said the most powerful book other than Scripture that I have ever read is Hans Küng's *On Being a Christian*. For me, no one has ever written or spoken with such passionate intelligence on the dark night of Jesus Christ. Here is a quote from this book:

> Jesus' unresisting suffering and helpless death, accursed and dishonored, for his enemies and even his friends, was the unmistakeable sign that he was finished and had nothing to do with the true God. His death on the cross was the fulfillment of the curse of the law. "Anyone hanged on a tree is cursed by God." He was wrong wholly and entirely: in his message, his behavior, his whole being. His claim is now refuted, his authority gone, his way shown to be false.... The heretical teacher is condemned, the false prophet disowned, the seducer of the people

unmasked, the blasphemer rejected. The law had triumphed over this "gospel."

Jesus found himself left alone, not only by his people, but by the One to whom he had constantly appealed as no one did before him. Left absolutely alone. We do not know what Jesus thought and felt as he was dying. But it was obvious to the whole world that he had proclaimed the early advent of God in his kingdom and this God did not come. A God who was man's friend, knowing all his needs, close to him, but this God was absent. A Father whose goodness knew no bounds, providing for the slightest things and the humblest people, gracious and at the same time mighty; but this Father gave no sign, produced no miracles.

His Father indeed, to whom he had spoken with a familiarity closer than anyone else had ever known, with whom he had lived and worked in a unity beyond the ordinary, whose true will he had learned with immediate certainty and in the light of which he had dared to assure individuals of the forgiveness of their sins; this Father of his did not say a single word. Jesus, God's witness, was left in the lurch by the God to whom he had witnessed. The mockery at the foot of the cross underlined vividly this wordless, helpless, miracle-less and even God-less death.

The unique communion with God which he had seemed to enjoy only makes his forsakenness more unique. This God and Father with whom he had identified himself to the very end did not at the end identify himself with the sufferer. And so everything seemed as if it had never been: in vain. He who had announced the closeness and advent of God his Father publicly before the whole world died utterly forsaken by God and was thus publicly demonstrated as godless before the whole world: someone judged by God himself, disposed of once and for all. And since the cause for which he had lived and fought was so closely linked to his person, so that cause fell with his person. There was no cause independent of his person. How could anyone have believed his word after he had been silenced and died in this outrageous fashion? It is a death not simply accepted in patience but endured screaming to God.[8]

A graphic description of the dark night of Jesus Christ. No human mind will ever comprehend the depths of desolation, the indescribable loneliness, the utter abandonment that lay behind Jesus' cry, *"Eloi, Eloi, lama sabachthani*—my God, my God, why have you forsaken me?" The cross is both the symbol of our salvation and the pattern of our lives. Everything that happened to Christ in some way happens to us. When darkness envelops us and we are deaf to everything except the shriek of our own pain, it helps to know that the Father is tracing in us the image of his Son, that the signature of Jesus is being stamped on our souls.

For Jesus the darkness of night gave way to the light of morning: "God highly exalted Him, and bestowed on Him the name which is above every name, so that at the name of Jesus every knee will bow, of those who are in heaven and on earth and under the earth, and that every tongue will confess that Jesus Christ is Lord, to the glory of God the Father" (Philippians 2:9–11, NASB).

Forgiveness is the key to everything. It forms the mind of Christ within us and prevents the costly and painful process of the dark night from itself becoming an ego trip. It guards us from feeling so "spiritually advanced" that we look down on those who are still enjoying the comforts and consolations of the first conversion. The gentle and humble in heart have the mind of Christ.

Henri Nouwen tells the story of an old man who used to meditate early every morning under a big tree on the bank of the Ganges. One morning, after he had finished his meditation, the old man opened his eyes and saw a scorpion floating helplessly in the water. As the scorpion was washed closer to the tree, the old man quickly stretched himself out on one of the long roots that branched out into the river and reached out to rescue the drowning creature. As soon as he touched it, the scorpion stung him. Instinctively the man withdrew his hand. A minute later, after he had regained his balance, he stretched himself out again on the roots to save the scorpion. This time the scorpion stung him so badly with its poisonous tail that his hand became swollen and bloody and his face contorted with pain.

At that moment, a passerby saw the old man stretched out on the roots struggling with the scorpion and shouted, "Hey, stupid old man, what's wrong with you? Only a fool would risk his life for the sake of an ugly, evil creature. Don't you know you could kill yourself trying to save that ungrateful scorpion?"

The old man turned his head. Looking into the stranger's eyes he said calmly, "My friend, just because it is the scorpion's nature to sting, that does not change my nature to save."

Sitting here at the typewriter in my study, I turn to the symbol of the crucified Christ on the wall to my left. And I hear Jesus praying for his murderers, "Father, forgive them. They do not know what they are doing."

The scorpion he had tried to save finally killed him. To me, the passerby, who sees him stretched out on the tree roots and shouts, "Only a madman would risk his life for the sake of an ugly, ungrateful creature," Jesus answers, "My friend, just because it is fallen mankind's nature to wound, that does not change my nature to save."

Here is the final repudiation of the ego. We surrender the need for vindication, hand over the kingdom of self to the Father, and in the sovereign freedom of forgiving our enemies, celebrate the luminous darkness.

Chapter Eight

THE LOVE
of JESUS

Down the corridor of time Christians have attempted to cope with the overwhelming reality of the person of Jesus Christ. I define coping as "our personal response of adaptation or adjustment produced by the encounter with the real Jesus."

There is a tendency in every Christian mind to remake the Man of Galilee, to concoct the kind of Jesus we can live with, to project a Christ who confirms our preferences and prejudices. The great English poet John Milton, for example, framed an intellectual Christ who scorned common people as "a herd confused, a miscellaneous rabble who extol things vulgar."

The tendency to construct a Christ in our own terms of reference and to reject any evidence that challenges our life situations and assumptions is human and universal. For many hippies in the sixties, Jesus was much like themselves—an agitator and social critic, a drop-out from the rat race, a prophet of the counterculture. For many yuppies in the eighties, Jesus was the provider of the good life, the Lord of the spa, a driven young executive with a messianic mission, the prophet of prosperity and the chauffeured limousine. After all, didn't he promise us a hundredfold in this life?

Is either the hippie Jesus or the yuppie Jesus a faithful portrait of the courageous, dynamic, free, and demanding Jesus of the New Testament?

In the musical *Godspell* we are presented with a sunshine gospel where carnival innocence, marvelous humor, and youthful energy sing a lullaby to the soul and entice us into a world of no personal accountability. Its selective approach gives a rollicking but essentially false idea of the gospel message. The crucifixion is an embarrassing "theological necessity" to be hastily hurdled. The resurrection is reduced to a song, "Long Live God." What do we make of a gospel without the paschal mystery? Where is the signature of Jesus?

In his book *Jesus Now*, Malachi Martin surveys the historical distortions of Jesus through the ages. First, there is "Jesus Caesar." In his name the church combined wealth and political power with professed service to God, an unsacramental marriage of church and state where the Pope in his ermine cape and Caesar in silk toga banded together to build empires. We find the same unholy alliance in our nation's capital today as certain religious leaders stalk the corridors of power baptizing some politicians and blacklisting others, always claiming to find support in the teaching of Jesus.

"Jesus Apollo" came later: a romantic visionary, a beautiful human leader with no disturbing overtones. He became the hero of the charming and gifted gentlemen of the nineteenth and early twentieth centuries, thinkers like Henry David Thoreau and Ralph Waldo Emerson. But Jesus Apollo never dirtied his hands, never walked into a migrant worker camp in Miami or a slum in New York City. He was no Savior. He did not advocate a living wage, decent housing, civil rights, or care for the aged.

In every age and culture we tend to shape Jesus to our own image and make him over to our own needs in order to cope with the stress his unedited presence creates. "In a foxhole Jesus is a rescue squad; in a dentist's chair a painkiller; on exam day a problem-solver; in an affluent society a clean-shaven middle-of-the-roader; for a Central American guerilla a bearded revolutionary."[1] If we think of Jesus as the friend of sinners, the sinners are likely to be our kind of people. I know, for instance, that Jesus befriends alcoholics. My personal history and cultural conditioning make Jesus congenial and compassionate with selective sinners just like myself. I can cope with this Jesus.

Blaise Pascal wrote, "God made man in his own image and man returned the compliment." Through five decades I have seen Christians shaping Jesus in their own image— in each case a dreadfully small deity. In his classic work *Your*

God Is Too Small, J. B. Phillips enumerated several of the cari-
catures: Resident Policeman, Parental Hangover, Grand
Old Man, Meek-and-Mild, Heavenly Bosom, Managing
Director, God in a Hurry, God for the Elite, God Without
Godhead, etc.

The same tendency persists today in Christology, especially in the disciples of "Jesus Torquemada." In the fif-
teenth century they persecuted and tortured anyone who
dared to disagree with their limited interpretation of
Scripture. Torquemada, whose Spanish name means
"orthodoxy of doctrine," died an old man in 1498, responsible for two thousand burnings at the stake and the exiling
of 160,000 Jews from Spain as undesirable aliens—all for
the glory of God. Torquemadeans are alive and well today
in every Christian denomination and nondenomination.
The same mean-mindedness, jealousy, ostracism, and
hatred still divide the body of Christ.

In reply to his haunting question "Who do you say that
I am?" my own experience of Jesus Christ cries out, "You
are the Son of God, the revealer of the Father's love!" This
astonishing truth, that Jesus embodies for us a Father who
loves us even when we fail to love, is the Good News. The
revelation that we are loved in an incomparable way
empowers us to be fools for Christ, to celebrate the darkness under the signature of Jesus. "For Christ's love com-
pels us" (2 Corinthians 5:14).

However, my past twenty-five years of pastoral experience indicate that the stunning disclosure that God is love
has had negligible impact on the majority of Christians and
minimal transforming power. The problem seems to be

that either we don't know it or we know it but cannot accept it. Or we accept it but are not in touch with it. Or we are in touch with it but do not surrender to it.

In spite of our reluctance and resistance, the essence and novelty of the New Covenant is that the very law of God's being is love. Pagan philosophers like Plato and Aristotle had arrived through human reasoning at the existence of God, speaking of him in vague, impersonal terms such as the Uncaused Cause and the Immovable Mover. The prophets of Israel had revealed the God of Abraham, Isaac, and Jacob in a more intimate and passionate manner. But only Jesus revealed that God is a Father of incomparable tenderness, that if we take all the goodness, wisdom, and compassion of the best mothers and fathers who have ever lived, they would only be a faint shadow of the love and mercy in the heart of the redeeming God.

Christianity moves in a climate completely penetrated by love, and we are called to a life of discipleship compatible with it, not living at a pre-Christian level eyeing God solely in terms of laws, rules, and obligations. God is love. We are called by Jesus Christ into an intimate friendship in which one member is a human being and the other the eternal God. We are invited to personal dialogue with the Holy One who is unreservedly involved with us. In his own person Jesus radically affirmed that God is not indifferent to human suffering. Jesus is God's Word to the world saying, "See how I love you."

If anyone should ask you, "What is the one thing in life that is certain?" before saying, "Death and taxes," a disciple must answer, "The love of Christ." Not parents, not friends—even the finest and dearest—not art or science or philosophy or any product of human wisdom. Only the love of Jesus Christ made manifest on the cross is certain. We cannot even say, "God's love," because the truth that God is love we know ultimately only through the signature of Jesus.

Several years ago a group of five computer salesmen went from Milwaukee to Chicago for a regional sales convention. All were married and each assured his wife he would return home in ample time for dinner. The sales meeting ran late, and the five scurried out of the building and ran toward the train station. A whistle blew, signaling the imminent departure of the train. As the salesmen raced through the terminal, one of them inadvertently kicked over a slender table on which rested a basket of apples. A ten-year-old boy was selling apples to pay for his books and clothes for school. With a sigh of relief, the five clambered aboard the train, but the last felt a twinge of compassion for the boy whose apple stand had been overturned.

He asked one of the group to call his wife and tell her he would be a couple of hours late. He returned to the terminal and later remarked that he was glad he did. The ten-year-old boy was blind. The salesman saw the apples scattered all over the floor. As he gathered them up, he noticed that several were bruised or split. Reaching into his pocket, he said to the boy, "Here's twenty dollars for the apples we damaged. I hope we didn't spoil your day. God bless you."

As the salesman started to walk away, the blind boy called after him and asked, "Are you Jesus?"

Who is this Jesus who is a magnetic field for so many people and a stumbling block for others?

Jesus is the revealer of the nature of the Godhead. To paraphrase John's prologue: When all things began, the Word already was. The Word dwelt with God, and what God was, the Word was. In other words, if one looked at Jesus one saw God, for "he who has seen Me has seen the Father" (John 14:9, NASB). Jesus is the complete expression of God. Through him as through no one else, God spoke and acted. When one met him one was met and judged and saved by God. This is what the apostles bore witness to. In this man, in his life, death, and resurrection, they had experienced God at work.

For "God was in Christ reconciling the world to Himself" (2 Corinthians 5:19, NASB). God vested himself completely in the man, Jesus of Nazareth. In him all his fullness dwells. What God is, Christ is. "He who believes in Me, does not believe in Me but in Him who sent Me" (John 12:44, NASB). Jesus reveals God by being utterly transparent to him. What had been cloaked in mystery is clear in Jesus—that God is love. No man or woman has ever loved like Jesus Christ.

I believe that at some point in his human journey Jesus was seized by the power of a great affection and experienced the love of his Father in a way that burst all previous boundaries of understanding. Whatever the external manifestations were, the baptism of Jesus Christ in the River Jordan was an awesome personal experience. The heavens are split, the Spirit descends in the form of a dove, and Jesus hears the words, "You are my Son, whom I love; with you I am well pleased" (Mark 1:11). The Father speaks to him with words of tender love. Jesus' lifelong response, rising from the depths of his soul, is *Abba*—a term more intimate than Father, which after that day is ever at the heart of his prayer.

The Abba experience is the source and secret of Christ's being, his message, and manner of life. It can be appreciated only by those who share it. Until we meet the Father of Jesus ourselves and experience him to be a loving, forgiving Daddy, it is impossible to understand Jesus' teaching on love.

In order to comprehend his relentless tenderness and passionate love for us, we must always return to his Abba experience. Jesus experienced God as tender and loving, courteous and kind, compassionate and forgiving, as laughter of the morning and comfort of the night. *Abba*, a colloquial form of address used by little Jewish children toward their fathers and best translated "Papa" or "Daddy," opened up the possibility of undreamed-of, unheard-of intimacy with God. In any other great world religion it is unthinkable to address almighty God as "Abba."

> Many devout Moslems, Buddhists, and Hinduists are generous and sincere in their search for God. Many have had profound mystical experiences. Yet in spite of their immeasurable spiritual depth, they seldom or never come to know God as their Father. Indeed, intimacy with Abba is one of the greatest treasures Jesus has brought us.[2]

Nor, according to Joachim Jeremias, does "Abba" have any parallel in Hebrew literature—prophetic, apocalyptic, or any other kind. Jesus alone knew God as Daddy. "No one knows the Father except the Son and those to whom the Son chooses to reveal him" (Matthew 11:27).

Abba. The overtones of this small word will always escape us. Yet in it we sense the intense intimacy of Jesus with his Father. We touch the heart of his faith. We come to understand the mind of Christ.

The parables of divine mercy—the lost coin, the lost sheep, the lost son—are rooted in Jesus' own experience of his Father. He speaks in the light of this reality. These stories were intended not only to defend his notorious conduct with sinners, but to startle his critics by cracking through their conventional ways of thinking about God. Jesus skewered his opponents with words to this effect: "The harlots who have no imagined righteousness to protect will be dancing into the kingdom while you have your alleged virtue burnt out of you! Hear me well: I have come to announce the dawn of a new era of incredible generosity. Allow yourselves to be captivated by joy and wonder at the surpassing greatness of my Father's love for the lost; set it over against your own joyless, loveless, thankless, and self-righteous lives. Let go of your impoverished understanding of God and your circumscribed notion of morality. Cease from your loveless ways. Celebrate the homecoming of the lost and rejoice in my Father's munificence."

The proclamation of the kingdom was born from the

urgency in the heart of Jesus. It was crucial that he bring the Good News of the gospel of grace—if only people could realize their own belovedness, their lives would be transformed and a new kingdom would spring into being.

You and I not only are invited but actually *called* to enter into this warm and liberating experience of God as Abba. In Romans 8, Paul is explicit: "You have not received a spirit of slavery leading to fear again, but you have received a spirit of adoption as sons by which we cry out, 'Abba! Father!'" (Romans 8:15, NASB). We are privileged to share in the intimacy of Jesus with his Father. We are called to live and to celebrate the same freedom that made Jesus so attractive and authentic.

Recently, a twenty-seven-year-old recovering alcoholic came to me for counseling. He had been born and raised a Roman Catholic. He had been married six times. His life was a tragic story of waste and wandering, boozing and womanizing. He asked me to help him return to the church. Normally my first reaction would have been to assure him that Jesus welcomed home the lost sheep and then pass quickly into outlining the canonical process of getting his first marriage annulled on the grounds of emotional and spiritual immaturity, whereupon all his other marriages would also be canonically invalid. I would have urged him to confess his sins and afterward to go to Mass and receive Communion.

But I found that the old tapes weren't spinning in my head. I wasn't replaying the dry-souled juridical office of the "pastoral counselor." I looked beyond the technical problem the man had brought to me. What I saw was a twenty-seven-year-old kid, a child of the Father, whose life was filled with squalid choices and failed dreams. Alcoholism had torn his life apart, unraveled the fabric of any moral training he might have received. He was broken, alienated from himself and God. A stranger in a strange land.

Tears were rolling down my face. I reached out, embraced him, held him for a long time, and said, "I have a word for you from your brother Jesus: Welcome home."

He was sobbing and asked, "Tell me who Jesus is."

I told him about my own tarnished past and the Jesus I had met in my need. We prayed. He accepted Jesus as his Savior. Light broke into his darkness. Peace filled our hearts.

Later when I was alone, the specter of canonical irregularity rose before me, and I felt a twinge of guilt for not observing due process. A quiet calm came when I prayed, "Dear Jesus, if it's a fault for being too kind to a sinner, then it's a fault I learned from you. For you never scolded anyone or brandished the Law at anyone who came to you seeking understanding and mercy."

Further along in his ministry, Jesus would say, "The Father and I are one," indicating an intimacy of life and love that defies description. To Philip he would say, "He who sees me sees the Father." Jesus is the human face of God, with all the attitudes, attributes, and characteristics of the Father.

So many Christians I know stop at Jesus. They remain on the Way without going where the Way leads them—to the Father. They want to be brothers and sisters without being sons and daughters. In them, the lament of Jesus is fulfilled: "Father of goodness and truth the world has not known you" (John 17:25, Phillips).

As the Father loved him, so Jesus would love us and invite us to do the same. "Love one another as I have loved you."

Jesus challenges us to forgive everyone we know and even those we don't know and to be very careful not to forget even one against whom we harbor ill will. Right now someone exists who has disappointed and offended us, someone with whom we are continually displeased and with whom we are more impatient, irritated, unforgiving, and spiteful than we would dare be with anyone else. That person is ourselves. We are so often fed up with ourselves. We're sick of our own mediocrity, revolted by our own inconsistency, bored by our own monotony. We would never judge any other of God's children with the savage self-condemnation with which we crush ourselves. Jesus said we are to love our neighbor as ourselves. We must be patient, gentle, and compassionate with ourselves in the same way we try to love our neighbor. I must be with Brennan what I was with the twenty-seven-year-old recovering alcoholic.

Through an intimate, heartfelt knowledge of Jesus Christ we learn to forgive ourselves. To the extent that we allow his kindness, patience, and trust toward us to win us over, we'll be freed from that dislike of ourselves that follows us everywhere. It is simply not possible to know the love of Jesus for us unless we alter our opinions and feelings about ourselves and side with him in his all-accepting love for us. Christ's forgiveness reconciles us with him, with ourselves, and with the whole community. According to

Bernard Bush, one way to know how Jesus feels about you is this: If you love yourself intensely and freely, then your feelings about yourself correspond perfectly to the sentiments of Jesus.

Jesus' intimacy with Abba God is translated into an intimate relationship with his disciples. He draws near to us and speaks in words of intense familiarity: "My little children, I shall not be with you much longer.... I will not leave you orphans. I will come back for you. I am going to prepare a place for you, and I shall return to take you with me." The Jesus who speaks here is not just a teacher or a model for us to imitate. He offers himself to each of us as a companion for the journey, as a friend who is patient with us, kind, never rude, quick to forgive, and whose love keeps no score of wrongs.

This is a beautiful dimension of discipleship, and Jesus lays great stress on it: "I stand at the door and knock. If anyone hears my voice and opens the door, I will come in and eat with him, and he with me" (Revelation 3:20). "If anyone loves me, he will obey my teaching. My Father will love him, and we will come to him and make our home with him" (John 14:23). "I no longer call you servants.... Instead, I have called you friends" (John 15:15).

St. Augustine said about this last verse, "A friend is someone who knows everything about you and still accepts you." This is the dream we all share: that one day I may meet the person to whom I can really talk, who will understand me and the words I say, and even hear what is left unsaid—and still will go on liking me.[3] Jesus Christ is the fulfillment of this dream.

Several years ago I wrote:

A friend is someone who stays with you in the bad
weather of life, guards you when you are off your
guard, restrains your impetuosity, delights in your
presence, forgives your failures, does not forsake
you when others let you down, and shares whatever
he or she might be having for breakfast (as Jesus
did on the beach along the Sea of Tiberias)—fish
and chips, moon pie, cold pizza, or chocolate cake
and milk.

As the old hymn reminds us, what a friend we have in
Jesus! A reality that dizzies the mind and dazzles the imagination! The beloved Son of the Father wants us to know,
to realize, and experience our own belovedness: "As the
Father has loved me, so have I loved you" (John 15:9).

Is this sense of belovedness real to you? Or has it
become jaded through repetition? Or like a knife slashing
through wallpaper, has it led to a dramatic breakthrough
into intimacy with God? A few years ago when I was in San
Jose, California, a woman of about thirty-five came up to
me and said, "We've never met, but I want you to know
that the sentence at the top of page eighty in your book *A
Stranger to Self-Hatred* changed my life." When I asked her
what the sentence was, she quoted from memory: "Jesus
loves us as we are and not as we should be, since none of us
is as we should be."

The life of Paul is anchored in his intimate friendship
with Jesus. "For living to me means simply 'Christ'"

(Philippians 1:21, Phillips). Daily, Paul turns his life over to Jesus, trusts him, praises him, asks him for what he needs, finds his *raison d'être* in him, and gratefully receives his love, which knows no shadow of change. He "loved me and gave Himself up for me" (Galatians 2:20, NASB). Never let these words be interpreted as mere intellectualizing by Paul. The love of Jesus Christ was a burning and divine reality for him, and his life is incomprehensible except in terms of it. Paul would have been buried in history as an unknown zealot except for his immense, uncompromising love for the person of Jesus. If you approached Paul and wanted to discuss parish renewal or contemporary worship, he would answer, "I have no understanding of church or religion except in terms of the sacred man Jesus who loved me and delivered himself up for me."

Paul uses the phrase "in Christ" one hundred and sixty-four times in his letters to describe what discipleship is all about. He is a powerful witness to the connectedness Jesus described in his farewell discourse: "I am the vine; you are the branches. If a man remains in me and I in him, he will bear much fruit; apart from me you can do nothing" (John 15:5).

The vine is the most intimate of all plants, growing over itself, into and around itself, intricately connected with all its parts. Jesus' image, "I am the vine," is the perfect expression of intimacy.

The paternal love of Abba is revealed as fraternal love in our brother Jesus. What depths of intimacy we are invited to! Prayer is simply relaxing and delighting in Jesus with no agenda except celebrating the deep affection between you. This interpersonal encounter deepens the sense of our own belovedness and alters our relationships with others.

We tend to restrict our warmth and acceptance to a selected few. But Jesus deepens human friendship as he deepens everything he touches. Without him, we find it difficult to relate to some people in a loving and respectful way. A certain stiffness coupled with a critical attitude prevent us from offering what these people need most—encouragement for their lives. But the friendship of Jesus enables us to see others as he saw the Twelve: flawed but good, wounded healers, children of the Father. We discover that we are compatible with a wide spectrum of people with whom we used to be uncomfortable and begin to pray, as Thomas Merton did, "I thank you, God, that I am like the rest of men."

I am writing these words in a chilly, dimly lit cabin tucked away in the Santa Cruz Mountains of northern California. If you picture the letter V, my cabin is right at the bottom of the valley where the diagonal lines converge—the lines represent the mountains that tower on both sides. I've been here for six days in silence and solitude. This retreat has been a journey from absurdity to obedience. Absurd comes from the Latin *surdus*, meaning "deaf." Obedience comes from the Latin *ob audire*, meaning "to listen to." Our busy world too often makes us deaf to the voice of God who speaks to us in silence.

Thus it is not surprising that we often wonder, in the midst of our occupied and preoccupied lives, if anything is really happening. Our lives may be filled to overflowing—so many events and commitments that we wonder how we'll get it all done. Yet at the same time, we might feel unfulfilled and wonder if anything is worth living for. Being filled yet unfulfilled, busy yet bored, involved yet lonely, these are the symptoms of the absurd lifestyle that makes us inattentive to spiritual realities.

I came here to listen to the Voice whispering in nature, in Word and sacrament, in the people who have crossed my path and touched my life. Today I wandered along a nature trail through a dense redwood forest humming aloud, "When through the woods and forests glades I wander...." I have a vivid image of myself staring up at one-hundred-fifty-foot redwoods in stillness, feeling tiny and insignificant and whispering, "How great thou art! O Abba, who is man that you should be mindful of him?"

I have a sad confession to make: Until this week I have never been able to experience God in natural beauty. Something undeveloped or broken inside of me, or perhaps trapped subconsciously in a mindset that says only useful things could and superfluous things like redwoods and roses are unimportant, has rendered me insensitive to finding God in nature. However, the love of a little Pomeranian puppy named Binky-Boo, whom I reluctantly allowed into our home for the sake of our daughter Nicole, has opened me up to discovering God's presence in creation and finding with Shakespeare "tongues in trees, books in the running brooks, sermons in stones and good in everything."[4]

At night I have been staring, shivering, up at the stars. There is a freshness about finding the Milky Way when you haven't seen it for a while. The stars call us out of ourselves. During this retreat I have read the Gospel of John and eight of Paul's letters. In my journal I have jotted down different things like "No one has ever seen God; it is only the Son who is nearest to the Father's heart who has made him known," and "God loved us with so much love that he was generous with his mercy; when we were dead through our sins, he brought us to life with Christ."

This is my last night in the cabin. I have prayed over John 21:15–17. Three times Jesus asks Peter, "Do you love me?" Instantly I identify with Peter, for my life has been the story of an unfaithful man through whom God continues to work. This is a word of consolation and liberation for me and anyone caught up in the oppressive notion that Jesus works only through the 100-percenters, that discipleship must be an untarnished success story. It is a word of healing for those of us who have painfully discovered that we are earthen vessels in whom Jesus' prophecy to Peter has been fulfilled: "This night, before the cock crows twice, you will have disowned me three times."

I completed the prayer time, packed my suitcase, turned toward the door, and suddenly in faith I saw the risen Jesus with the holes, the wounds of love, in his hands and feet and side. I wept aloud. His warmth and affection came crashing down. It was overwhelming. I knew that I have not begun to know. Everything I have ever written, spoken, or experienced of the love of Jesus Christ is barely a hint, a straw, or dry leaves blowing in the wind.

In faith I heard him say, "Three times I have asked, 'Do you love me?' Now face your shadow. Look carefully at what you most despise in yourself and then look through it. At your center you will discover a love for me beyond words, images, and concepts—a love you are unable to understand or contain. Your love for me is fragile but real. Trust it."

It is only this wounded Jesus who provides the final revelation of God's love. The crucified Christ is not an abstraction but the ultimate answer to how far love will go, what measure of rejection it will endure, how much self-ishness and betrayal it will withstand. The unconditional love of Jesus Christ nailed to the wood does not flinch before our perversity. "He took up our infirmities and car-ried our diseases" (Matthew 8:17).

In 1960 a pastor in East Germany wrote a play called *The Sign of Jonah*. The last scene dealt with the final judg-ment. All the peoples of the earth are assembled on the plain of Jehoshaphat awaiting God's verdict. They are not, however, waiting submissively; on the contrary, they are gathered in small groups, talking indignantly. One group is a band of Jews, a sect that has known little but religious, social, and political persecution throughout their history. Included in their number are victims of Nazi extermina-tion camps. Huddled together, the group demands to know what right God has to pass judgment on them, espe-cially a God who dwells eternally in the security of heaven.

Another group consists of American blacks. They, too, question the authority of God who never has experienced the misfortunes of men, never known the squalor and depths of human degradation to which they were subjected in the suffocating holds of slave ships. A third group is composed of persons born illegitimately, the butt of jokes and sneers all their lives.

Hundreds of such groups are scattered across the plain: the poor, the afflicted, the maltreated. Each group appoints a representative to stand before the throne of God and challenge his divine right to pass sentence on their immortal destinies. They meet in council and decide that this remote and distant God who has never experienced human agony is unqualified to sit in judgment unless he is willing to enter into the suffering, humiliated state of man and endure what they have undergone.

Their conclusion reads: "You must be born a Jew; the circumstances of your birth must be questioned; you must be misunderstood by everyone, insulted and mocked by your enemies, betrayed by your friends; you must be persecuted, beaten, and finally murdered in a most public and humiliating fashion."

Such is the judgment passed on God by the assembly. The clamor rises to fever pitch as they await his response. Then a brilliant, dazzling light illuminates the entire plain. One by one, those who have passed judgment on God fall silent. For emblazoned high in the heavens for the whole world to see is the signature of Jesus Christ with this inscription above it: "I have served my sentence."

Chapter Nine

THE DISCIPLINE
of THE SECRET

AN OPEN LETTER TO AMERICAN CHRISTIANS
ANYWHERE, USA

*D*EAR BROTHERS AND SISTERS IN THE LORD JESUS,
   Over the past several years my ministry as a vagabond
evangelist has moved me into a wide ecumenical network.
I have preached the gospel in evangelical, charismatic, and
mainline churches, as well as college campuses, presidential
prayer breakfasts, medical meetings, and weekend retreats.
From Sacramento to St. Petersburg and from Chicago to
Chula Vista, I am repeatedly asked the same question:
"Brennan, based on your exposure to such a broad spec-
trum of Christian communities, how would you describe

the spiritual state of the American church, and do you have any recommendations for reform and renewal?"

You have encouraged me not to mince words or resort to sensitive soul-blubber. In reply, I write this open letter to American Christians and submit the following reflections and recommendations.

As we make our way into the twenty-first century, there never has been a time in Christian history when the name of Jesus Christ so frequently is mentioned and the content of his life and teaching so frequently ignored. The seduction of counterfeit discipleship has made it too easy to be a Christian. In a climate of mutual admiration, the radical demands of the gospel have dissolved into verbal Alka-Seltzer, and prophetic preaching has become virtually impossible. By and large, American Christians today are spoon-fed the pabulum of popular religion.

The gospel of Jesus Christ is no Pollyanna tale for the neutral—it is a cutting knife, rolling thunder, and convulsive earthquake in the human spirit. The Word should force us to reassess the entire direction of our lives. But in the words of Bonhoeffer, many Christians "have gathered like ravens around the carcass of cheap grace and there have drunk the poison which has killed the following of Christ."

If the gospel were proclaimed without compromise, the roster of card-carrying Christians in this country would shrink. Most televangelism distorts the gospel. There is no reference to the Cross except as a theological relic, no clarion call to the body of Christ that we are crucified to the world and the world to us. In a half hour the electronic evangelist has to convert you, heal you, and guarantee your success. Everybody is a winner; nobody loses his business, fails in marriage, or lives in poverty. If you are an attractive nineteen-year-old and accept Jesus, you become Miss America; if you have a drinking problem, you conquer alcoholism; if you are in the National Football League, you automatically go to the Pro Bowl.

Incredible as it may sound, the Word itself has become a source of division and self-righteousness. Jesus said that the foremost sign of discipleship would be our love for one another: "A new command I give you: Love one another. As I have loved you, so you must love one another. By this all men will know that you are my disciples, if you love one another" (John 13:34–35). His teaching is unequivocal here. We would be known as his followers not because we are chaste, celibate, honest, sober, or respectable; not because we are church-going, Bible-toting, or Psalm-singing. Rather, we would be recognized as disciples primarily by our deep and delicate respect for one another, our cordial love impregnated with reverence for the sacred dimension of the human personality.

However, in an arrogant gesture of one-upmanship, many preachers today have decided that Jesus' standard for discipleship is inadequate for modern times. The new criterion is orthodoxy of doctrine coupled with the way we interpret the Bible. "Right thinking" is the new norm for determining what a Christian is worth. In these parlous times we do not shrink from splitting up fellowship, local churches, and even denominations over the form of worship, the songs we sing, or the method of interpreting a Bible passage.

My friends in Christ, the simple truth is that the Christian church in America is divided by doctrine, history, and day-to-day living. We have come a long, sad journey from the first century when pagans exclaimed with awe and wonder, "See how these Christians love one another!" to the twenty-first century when all over the world nonbelievers dismiss us with contempt: "See how these Christians hate one another!" We have deprived the world of the only witness the Son of God asked for during the supper of his love. "Our present disunity cannot be God's will for us; it is a scandal to angels in heaven and human beings on earth."[1]

However, let me say that across this country there is a congregation here, a small community there, isolated witnesses on the horizon whose lives make no sense whatsoever if Jesus is not risen. They see Christianity not as a ritual but as a way of life. Their lives off-camera are impressive. They do things that no one can ever possibly know about with the same sincerity as they do the things that people can see. They have staked everything on the signature of Jesus, and they firmly believe that to live without risk is to risk not living.

I am deeply distressed by what I can only call in our Christian culture the idolatry of the Scriptures. For many Christians, the Bible is not a pointer to God but God himself. In a word—bibliolatry. God cannot be confined within the covers of a leather-bound book. I develop a nasty rash around people who speak as if mere scrutiny of its pages will reveal precisely how God thinks and precisely what God wants.

The four Gospels are the key to knowing Jesus. But conversely, Jesus is the key to knowing the meaning of the gospel—and of the Bible as a whole. Instead of remaining content with the bare letter, we should pass on to the more profound mysteries that are available only through intimate and heartfelt knowledge of the person of Jesus.[2]

At the risk of sounding repetitious, I shall say it again: We have made it too easy to be a Christian. The sole requirements are the recitation of a creed and attendance at a local church where there is no community and little fellowship. Christianity used to be risky business. It is no longer. Cost-free discipleship produces wimps and pleasant personalities who, in Scott Peck's forceful phrase, "belong to a church that in the name of Jesus can blasphemously co-exist with the arms race."[3]

From my vantage point, the greatest single need in the American church is to know Jesus Christ, to live and breathe the words of the apostle Paul: "All I want is to know Christ and to experience the power of his resurrection through sharing in the fellowship of his suffering" (see Philippians 3:10–11). You and I are called to be persons after the manner of Jesus. *Nothing else matters.* Our goal is to become as Christ, to always have his image before our eyes. Discipleship is a complete attachment to Jesus Christ in his present risenness: "Let us fix our eyes on Jesus, the author and perfecter of our faith" (Hebrews 12:2). We must be totally focused on Christ, looking neither to law nor to church membership nor to personal piety nor to personal success in ministry nor to career advancement nor to the world for fulfillment. "Christ is all, and is in all" (Colossians 3:11).

Paul is a model of single-minded dedication to Jesus. He had the audacity to boast, "We have the mind of Christ" (I Corinthians 2:16). His boast was validated by his life. From the moment of his conversion, Paul's mind and heart were preoccupied with Jesus Christ (see Philippians 3:21). Christ was a person whose voice Paul could recognize (see 2 Corinthians 13:30), who strengthened him in his moments of weakness (see 2 Corinthians 12:9), who enlightened him, showed him the meaning of things, and consoled him (see 2 Corinthians 1:4–5). Driven to desperation by the slanderous charges of false apostles, Paul admitted to visions and revelations of the Lord Jesus (see 2 Corinthians 12:1). The person of Jesus unraveled for him the mystery of life and death (see Colossians 3:3).

In the novel *To Kill A Mockingbird,* the old lawyer Atticus Finch says, "You'll never understand a man 'til you stand in his shoes and look at the world through his eyes." Paul looked at the world so sensitively through the eyes of Jesus Christ that Christ became the ego of the apostle: "I have been crucified with Christ and I no longer live, but Christ lives in me" (Galatians 2:20).

If the apostle were to return to earth today, I believe he would call the entire American church to return to *the discipline of the secret*. This ancient practice of the apostolic church was implemented to protect the sacred name of Jesus Christ from mockery and the mysteries of the

Christian faith from profanation. The ancient church avoided mention of baptism, Eucharist, and the death and resurrection of Christ in the presence of the unbaptized.[4] Why? Because the most persuasive witness was the way one lived, not the words one spoke.

Søren Kierkegaard once described two types of Christians: The first group comprises those who imitate Jesus Christ; the second are those who are content to speak about him. I would divide the Christian community in the United States into the *picture people* and the *drama people*. The picture people view Jesus safely and from a distance, as one would view Salvador Dali's painting of the Last Supper at the National Gallery of Art in Washington, D.C. The drama people are not spectators but, like the audience caught up in the Greek tragedy *Antigone,* are personal participants in the drama of Jesus' death and resurrection through a daily dying to self in order to rise to newness of life with Christ.

I propose that the Christian enterprise of building the kingdom of God on earth must be a silent, hidden affair. The public claims of many Christians have lost their credibility. The words on their lips are contradicted by their lifestyles.

The problem in the American church is not that something has been hidden but that not enough has stayed hidden. Let the church go underground for a while. As it lowers its profile, let it raise the ante for membership. We are the church. Let us present to the world the image of a servant community, and let us preserve the beauty of the gospel not with showy, defensive fervor but with an intense interior life of prayer and worship, service, and a manner of living that only can be explained in terms of God.

Worship is the summit of the church's life, the fount of all ministry, the shared solidarity in community that makes fidelity to Jesus possible. Worship, as an expression of the discipline of the secret, is not for dilettantes seeking entertainment.

> It is only for small groups of clearly committed Christians who comprise an intense community on the basis of their common, intense loyalty to Christ; and their expression of the meaning of that loyalty and community is communicated to and with one another in worship.... Worship as arcane discipline is not for the streets, for the posters, for the media, for the masses. It certainly is not the Hollywood Bowl and drive-in Easter sunrise services, nor Sunday East Room exercises in American civil religion, nor Astrodome rallies or religiosity.... It is not bumper- sticker and slick-paper Christianity. The church...will be rigorous in its membership stipulations and devout in its practice of disciplines. It will also give up its property for the sake of the needy.[5]

The discipline of the secret will help the American church become liberated from religiosity. We are carrying a lot of religious baggage from the past. In several local churches I have visited, religiosity has pushed Jesus to the margins of real life and plunged people into preoccupation with their own personal salvation. When fear of sin and death dominates the Christian consciousness, we become excessively introspective; we take our eyes off Jesus and lose any sense of ethical responsibility to the broader human community. Many people have confused the structures of religion with revelation and faith. The discipline of the secret insists that Jesus not only is the center of the gospel but of our entire Christian life. Only allegiance to him and imitation of his life will make Christianity credible.

Overuse has rendered much of Christian language meaningless. When you encounter someone in grief or desolation, do not speak the biblical language known to you and available to you: stand with the wounded man or woman in his or her loneliness and brokenness, weep and mourn with them, and let your silence be your compassion.

I remind every follower of Jesus that discipleship means nothing less than being ready to obey Christ as unconditionally as the first disciples. Only he who believes is obedient, and only he who is obedient believes. Never confuse success in ministry or knowledge of the Bible or mastery of Christian principles and ideas with holiness and authentic discipleship. They may well be the corruption of discipleship if your life is not hidden with Christ in God.

A remarkable old woman named Catherine de Hueck Doherty (often called the "Baroness" because she had married a Russian baron) was both street-smart from years of ministry to the downtrodden in New York City and a true contemplative. (Read her book *Poustinia*—Russian for "hermitage.") At the end of her life, she wrote, "It seems as if the world needs fools—fools for Christ! For it is such fools that have changed the face of the earth."

I invite you to join the cadre of Christian fools whom Jesus of Nazareth is raising up in this new century. The ranks of the cadre transcend all class distinctions between male and female, progressive and conservative, charismatic and traditional, clergy and laity, young and old. All differences dissolve in the unifying love of the Spirit (see Galatians 3:28). The sole requirements for membership are the experiential awareness of Jesus as saving Lord, surrender to the sway of the Holy Spirit, and stable commitment to the mission of building the new heavens and the new earth under the signature of Jesus.

A word of caution: The cadre of fools for Christ will disturb the establishment because they stand as a sign of contradiction to the compromises many Christians have married. You will untack the liberal tailors because you refuse to cut your conscience to fit this year's fashion. You will worry the palace guard because they are serving another. You will vex the museum watchmen—if you have the pearl, they are guarding an empty vault. Most distressing of all, if you have the Truth, *every man's life is a lie.*

Living by the discipline of the secret, you will give offense. This is bound to be so (see John 15:18). Today Christianity is largely inoffensive, and this kind of religion never will transform anything. Because you refuse to buy into "cheap grace" that keeps faith solely on the intellectual level, refusing to dirty its Christian hands with the messy problems besetting church and country, you will be called bad names and perhaps much worse. Jesus Christ offended the religious and political order of Palestine. The Christian, too, is bound to give offense, and if he or she does not, it is a bad sign—it means they cannot be very Christian.

In this letter, dear brothers and sisters, I have shared my own perception of the church in America and offered recommendations for renewal based on the writings of Paul. At this moment in church history, I believe that the return to the discipline of the secret is essential to the revitalization and credibility of the Christian community, USA. The gospel of Jesus Christ is not to be forced upon an unwilling world. To put it bluntly, people have had their bellyful of our sermonizing. They want a source of strength for their lives. We can recommend it only by making it actively present in our own. In terms of church growth for the next decade, the operative principle is "less is more." Shortly before his death, the Marxist leader Lenin said, "Give me ten men like Francis of Assisi and I will rule the world."

Please pray for this pilgrim. I do not stand above you; I sit beside you.

Under the Mercy,
Brennan Manning
New Orleans, Louisiana
January 15, 1992

Chapter Ten

THE COURAGE
to RISK

THE STORY OF THE FIRST Pentecost is a familiar one. Fifty days after Easter, the disciples were gathered together in one place. Suddenly they were engulfed in a mighty wind and startled by flames of fire resting on each of them. Filled with the Spirit and power, they were able to speak to Passover pilgrims from many lands and be understood in their local languages. Though dramatic, this story is easy to follow and also to visualize.

Whenever the Spirit of God breaks into our lives—in the middle of the day, in the middle of the week, or the middle of a lifetime—it is to announce in some fashion that the time for pussyfooting is over. The mighty rushing wind of the first Pentecost symbolized that something new and wonderful was coming to pass by the power of God. Just as a band of timid, evasive, and helpless disciples were transformed into fearless, articulate witnesses, so with us. When we are seized by the power of a great affection, we are empowered with the courage to risk. The Spirit sets us free from our self-imposed limits and moves us out into uncharted waters. Our secure, well-regulated, and largely risk-free lives are blown apart. The Spirit saves us from "both our high idealism (with all its ego investment) and our low self-esteem (with its even more intense ego investment) and lifts us beyond our utmost bounds to undreamed-of possibilities, to the idealism of God himself."[1]

Prior to the Pentecost, the track record of the Twelve was poor: They had complained, they had quarreled, they had wavered, they had deserted. The biography of these apostolic stalwarts was one of wary, inconsistent discipleship. Yet God's free use of flawed people to accomplish his purposes is a resounding affirmation to those of us trapped in feelings of inadequacy and inferiority. As Alan Jones has noted, "The most difficult thing in mature believing is to accept that I am an object of God's delight."

More often than I like to admit, I still get bamboozled into trying to make myself acceptable to God. It seems I cannot forgo this crazy enterprise of getting myself into a position where I can see myself in a good light. I still struggle to let go of the preposterous pretense that my paltry prayers, knowledge of Scripture, spiritual insights, tithing to the poor, and blustering successes in ministry endear me to God's eyes. I resist the saving truth that I am lovable simply and solely because he loves me.

Anyone caught up in the same oppression of self-justification understands what I am saying. In our own way we are as absurd as the character in the Agatha Christie novel who cannot imagine heaven as being anything but an occasion to make herself useful, little imagining that everybody else in heaven may be struggling to endure the unceasing persecution of her devoted service. Will we ever be free of the Pelagian fantasy that we save ourselves?

In pensive moments I wonder if I really have the courage to risk everything on the gospel of grace and accept the total sufficiency of Christ's redeeming work. My futile attempts at self-improvement, the sadness that I am not yet perfect, the boasting about my victories in the vineyard, my sensitivity to criticism, and the lack of self-acceptance belie my profession of faith that Jesus is Lord—lip service from a shackled servant still in bondage to the insecurity that wears a thousand masks, still lacking the courage to risk all on him who is all, still thrashing about trying to fix myself, still struggling for that elusive achievement that will make me presentable to God. Brennan the basket case!

False modesty? No, otherwise why was I rattled when, after a sermon I preached in Chapel Hill, North Carolina, evangelist Tommy Tyson looked up with tears in his eyes and said, "Something wonderful just happened to me: I know as I have never known before that what Jesus did was enough."

On that overcast afternoon I decided to put my do-it-yourself kit in a garage sale, jettison some heavy cargo I had been carrying, and hearken to the words of Robert M.

Brown: "Be it hereby enacted: That every three years all people shall forget whatever they have learned about Jesus, and begin the study all over again."[2]

The Spirit convicted Peter that he was not doomed to repeat the mistakes of the past. Nor are we. There is a power available to transcend our automatic emotional responses and robot-like behavior. Endowed with the courage to risk everything on the truth of the gospel, we surrender our gnawing need to be okay and cease applying spiritual cosmetics to make ourselves presentable.

And yet…the prospect frightens us. We'd like to stay close enough to the fire to keep warm but are reluctant to dive in. We know we will come out burnt, incandescently transformed. Life never will be the same again. Nonetheless, we are dissatisfied with the narrow dimensions of our partial commitment. Deep within there is a longing to throw caution to the winds. We know that what Leon Bloy said is true: "The only real sadness in life is not to be a saint."

Graham Greene wrote a telling novel entitled *The Power and the Glory*. The central character is the "whiskey priest," a sad man, lax, tepid, and alcoholic. At the moment he is about to be executed by a firing squad, he realizes it would have been easy to be a saint if he had had the courage to risk. For years the inner robot had controlled his outer life. Looking into the barrels of five loaded rifles, he perceives that his weakness was only hypochondria. A few hours earlier, he had walked across this courtyard and nothing he saw seemed to matter. Long ago he had bartered courage and freedom for passivity and trivialities. Were his execution delayed and he could walk back across the courtyard, he would be wide-eyed with wonder. Puddles would seem like oceans, soldiers like gods. With his inner robot suppressed and his automatic emotions no longer in command, he would lay hold of his life, grasp it round the neck, and move in the conviction that to live without risk is to risk not living.

In the power of a great affection, the impossible becomes possible. We are freed from the fears that lock us. We know we can't lose because we have nothing *to* lose.

Nothing is more puzzling to me than our massive resistance to the inbreak of God's love. Why are we so churlish to receive? Are we afraid of becoming vulnerable, of losing control of our lives, of acknowledging our weakness and need? Do we keep God at a safe distance to protect the illusion of our independence?

The parable of the unforgiving debtor (see Matthew 18) offers a clue. He owes his master the sum of ten thousand talents—the equivalent of the national debt. What does he do? Does he cast himself on the mercy of his merciful master, admit his total helplessness in the situation, and beg forgiveness? Absolutely not. The debtor is not into admitting inadequacy. He is a man of substance and consequence. He has credentials and credit cards. Honors have been conferred upon him. His ego has been stroked. His dignity is intact.

In a preposterous statement, he says to his master: "Look here, you are a reasonable man. You know the stock market is mercurial. I just ran into a streak of bad luck. Give me a little time and I will repay the national debt." Being realistic, his master instead forgives the entire amount. But the debtor, of course, misses the freeing import of this incredible generosity. He hadn't asked for any favors! He'd been going to repay that impossible sum through his own efforts. And because he could not receive forgiveness, he could not extend it to his fellow servant who owed him a paltry sum.[3]

This false sense of self, brimming with pride and pretense, must die if we are to live. The constant challenge in this life we call Christian is the translation of what we believe into our day-to-day lifestyle. Risky business!

This doesn't, of course, mean conforming to some prescribed pattern of enthusiastic affection, such as a variety of modern movements are eager to impose. Rather, it is a thing of complete spontaneity, unprogrammed and unpredictable. It is more likely to make us feel foolish (if we are the least bit self-conscious) than to make us feel that at last we have arrived at Christian maturity. In order to do more than adopt a passing fad, we never forget that the spontaneous affection erupting within us is the love of God poured into our hearts by the Holy Spirit. The courage to risk approaching an enemy to seek reconciliation belongs in the same category. It will expose us to very probable rejection, ridicule, and failure.

In retrospect, the landmark moments in my life are not the gross sins I committed nor the infrequent acts of heroic virtue I performed, but a handful of decisions that involved risk: the decision to seek ordination to the priesthood, to join the Little Brothers of Jesus, to live in a cave, to seek help for my addiction to alcohol, to marry. On the last day, when we stand before the risen Christ, each of us will be the sum of our choices.

Mister Blue was a daring gentleman who lived at ease with music and balloons on an apartment house roof. He moved gracefully with all kinds of people in poverty and abundance and refused to be tied down to the standards of others. In the evening of his life, Mister Blue wrote:

> Conservative historians describe any man with a passion for greatness as a megalomaniac. "Look at him," they say to one another, "the idiot! Why doesn't he settle down and establish himself in the community? Why is he forever restless, forever trying to get something beyond him? The man is crazy."
>
> These conservatives are partly right. Play life safe and you will keep out of harm. Be careful, be cautious, don't take risks and you will never die on Mount St. Helens. Your failure is measured by your aspirations. Aspire not, and you cannot fail. Columbus died in chains. Joan of Arc was burned at the stake. Let us all live snugly without risk, and life will soon be little more than a thick gelatinous stream of comfortability and ignorance.[4]

The restlessness of the fictional Mister Blue echoes the parable of Jesus on the unprofitable servant (Luke 17:7–10). It recalls the deathbed exhortation of Francis of Assisi: "Let us begin, my brothers, for up to now we have done but little."

Blue can be heard in the gentle voice of my friend Tom Minifie, an associate pastor in Seattle: "To be at ease is to be unsafe." The church of the Lord Jesus starts to decay when the members who comprise it forfeit their willingness to risk.

Every college president recognizes that some academic departments are enjoying exceptional vitality while others drone along. Every businessman observes that some firms are on their toes while others are in a rut. The same factors are at work in the rise and fall of any enterprise, including the church's. Rome falling to the barbarians, an old family firm going into bankruptcy, a government agency strangling in its own red tape, a church dying of spiritual consumption—all have a great deal in common.

When an institution is young, it is flexible, fluid, willing to try anything once. As the institution ages, risk-taking decreases, daring gives way to rigidity, creativity fades, the capacity to meet new challenges from unexpected directions is lost.

The same processes at work in the demise of institutions likewise operate in the decline of individuals. "Why is it," John Gardner asks, "that so many people are mummified by the time of middle age?" Why do some people settle into rigid and unchanging views on God and church by the time they are thirty years old? Why do we fall into a stupor of mind and spirit long before we are golden girls and boys? Is it inevitable that we surrender our youthfulness and our capacity to grow and change? Is personal renewal, the seedbed of community renewal, possible?

Perhaps the major cause of failure in individual and community renewal is the very fear of failure itself. We avoid risk so as not to be shown up as mistaken before the world. The tyranny of our peers—what will others say?—

immobilizes us. Wise and prudent people that we are, we manufacture a thousand logical excuses for doing nothing.

The fear of falling on our faces exacts a heavy price. It discourages exploration and assures the progressive narrowing of the personality. There is no learning without fumbling. If we are to keep growing, we must risk failure all our lives. When Max Planck was awarded the Nobel Prize for the formulation of the quantum theory, he said, "Looking back over the long and labyrinthine path which finally led to the discovery, I am vividly reminded of Goethe's saying that men will always be making mistakes as long as they are striving after something."

Although Christianity is all about redemption from sin and failure, the majority of us (based on my pastoral experience) are unwilling to admit to failure in our lives. Partially this is due to human nature's defense mechanisms against its own inadequacies. Even more, it can be traced to the success image our current Christian culture demands of us. Once converted we no longer dare lose our businesses, our marriages, or our figures.

The problem with projecting the perfect image, however, is that it creates more problems than it solves. First, it is simply not true—none of us is always joyful, unruffled, and in command. Second, projecting the flawless image distances us from other people who conclude we would not understand them. Third, even if we could live a life free of risk and mistakes, it would be a shallow existence. Mature Christians are those who have failed and learned to live gracefully with their failure.

Our failure to have done with our lives what we longed

to accomplish weighs heavy on most of us. The disparity between our ideal self and our real self, the specter of past infidelities, the awareness that my behavior often flatly denies my beliefs, the pressure of conformity, and our nostalgia for lost innocence reinforce a nagging sense of existential guilt: I have failed. This is the cross we never expected, the one we find hardest to bear. We can no longer differentiate between our perception of ourselves and the mystery we really are.[5]

The pernicious myth "once converted, fully converted" creates the impression that in one blinding bolt of salvation Christ expects our lives to be freed from contradictions and perplexities. The curse of perfectionism triggers episodes of depression and anxiety. Who will acquit us of guilt? Who will deliver us from the bondage of perfectionism and failure? Once again, it is the signature of Jesus that rescues us from ourselves.

The crucified Christ reminds us that despair and disillusionment are not terminal but signs of impending resurrection. What lives beyond the Cross is the liberating power of love, freeing us from the ego-centeredness that says, *All I am is what I think I am and nothing more*. One Good Friday morning at 2:00 A.M., as I prayed in faith I heard him say, "Little brother, I witnessed a Peter who claimed that he did not know me, a James who wanted power in return for service, a Philip who failed to see the Father in me, and scores of disciples who were convinced I was finished on Calvary. The New Testament has many examples of men and women who started out well and then faltered along the way.

"Yet on Easter night I appeared to Peter; James is not remembered for his ambition but for the sacrifice of his life for the kingdom; Philip did see the Father in me when I pointed the way; and the disciples who despaired had enough courage to recognize me as the stranger who walked the road to Emmaus. My point, little brother, is this: I expect more failure from you than you expect from yourself."

In season and out of season, in success and failure, in grace and disgrace, the courage to risk everything on the signature of Jesus is the mark of authentic discipleship. In the words of Winston Churchill, "Success is never final; failure is never fatal. It is courage that counts."

Chapter Eleven

GRABBING AHOLT
of GOD

WILLIAM REISER WRITES, "Many parents have waited years for their children to acknowledge that they have been loved. There are many times, naturally, when mothers and fathers find their patience exhausted by children who seem to take them for granted and rarely give a thought to their parents' feelings. Yet, somehow, parents retain faith in their children because they believe that so much care and love must one day bear fruit. Parents live in hope for the day when a child will realize what love he has received. I remember a father confiding to me that he would give anything he had in order to have his son come home one day and throw his arms not around his father (that would have been too much to hope for) but around his mother and tell her, 'I love you.'"[1]

When children acknowledge the love that has been lavished on them, parents resonate to that acknowledgment of being appreciated with an inaudible sigh that ranks with the happiest moments of their lives and their marriage. Is it far-fetched to imagine God experiencing the same thing? Does he not long for children who gratefully acknowledge how deeply they have been loved?

One day Rabbi Barukh's grandson Yehiel was playing hide-and-seek with another boy. He hid himself well and waited for his playmate to find him. After twenty minutes, he peeked out of his secret hiding place, saw no one, and pulled his head back inside. After waiting a very long time, he came out of his hiding place, but the other boy was nowhere to be seen. Then Yehiel realized that his playmate had not looked for him from the very beginning. Crying, he ran to his grandfather and complained of his faithless friend. Tears brimmed in Rabbi Barukh's eyes as he realized that God says the same thing: *I hide but no one wants to seek me*.[2]

Such was the poignant tone of God's voice when he spoke through the mouth of his prophet Hosea:

"When Israel was a child, I loved him, and out of Egypt I called my son. But the more I called Israel, the further they went from me. They sacrificed to the Baals and they burned incense to images. It was I who taught Ephraim to walk, taking them by the arms; but they did not realize it was I who healed them. I led them with cords of human kindness, with ties of love; I lifted the yoke from their neck and bent down to feed them." (Hosea 11:1-4)

Our God remains a hidden God, but in prayer we discover that we have what we seek. We start from where we are, learn what we have, and realize we are already there. Contemplative prayer is simply experiencing what we already possess. "Don't you know that you yourselves are God's temple and that God's Spirit lives in you?" (1 Corinthians 3:16).

During a conference on contemplative prayer, the question was put to Thomas Merton, "How can we best help people to attain union with God?" His answer was very clear: We must tell them that they are already united with God. "Contemplative prayer is nothing other than 'coming into consciousness' of what is already there."[3]

Contemplative prayer is, as Tad Dunne once put it, the appreciation and realization of the *concrete* meaning of love. (It was my sponsor in Alcoholics Anonymous, Buzzy Gaiennie, who got me in touch with this definition.) The task of contemplative prayer is to help me achieve the conscious awareness of the unconditionally loving God dwelling within me. "What this means, in very practical terms, is that I don't have to worry about 'getting anywhere' in prayer, because I am already there. I simply have to become *aware* of this."[4]

As was stated in the opening chapter, the tragedy in the church today is that we have confused beliefs and faith, doctrines and lived experience. Contemplative prayer bridges the gap between belief and experience because it is the bridge of faith. It teaches us what theology alone could never convince us of—that God is love. It takes us on the longest and most dangerous journey of all, from the head to the heart wherein we taste and existentially experience the relentless tenderness of Jesus Christ. We come to *know* the compassion of Christ not as an abstraction but in the *lived experience* of his acceptance of us as sinners, as imperfect people caught up in a struggle in which we sometimes sell out ourselves or others. We experience the forgiveness of Jesus not as the reprieve of a judge but the embrace of a lover. We are liberated from pettiness, self-centeredness, and fear. We are purified in the darkness of faith, beyond belief.

"I don't see why anyone should settle for anything less than Jacob," writes Walker Percy, "who actually *grabbed aholt* of God and wouldn't let go until God identified himself and blessed him."[5]

"Grabbing aholt" of God is the goal of contemplative prayer. That is why the first step in faith is to stop thinking about God at the time of prayer. We have instead to believe—not just intellectually but with the totality of our being that makes belief into faith—that he is with us and we in him. "Remain in me, and I will remain in you" (John 15:4). Grabbing aholt of God in faith means simultaneously being seized by the power of a great affection of being grabbed aholt of.

"You will seek me and find me when you seek me with all your heart. I will be found by you" (Jeremiah 29:13–14). It is Yahweh who speaks.

In my personal life the greater part of each year is devoted to writing, thinking, and speaking about God, Jesus, faith, contemplative prayer, the gospel lifestyle, and so forth. It is a curious phenomenon that such noble Christian enterprises distance me from God. (I assume that this is true for all Christian writers, preachers, and teachers, as well as songwriters, musicians, and singers.) Constantly holding forth *about* God does not of itself lead to being *with* God. Writing *about* God somehow takes me away from directly responding to God in the present moment. Preaching *about* Jesus somehow clouds my presence to the Reality I am proclaiming. In both situations, what is missing is any sense of felt intimacy with God through faith. Yet my beliefs remain vigorous and rooted.

In the Gospels, Scripture scholars tell us that there is not a single passage in which the Greek word for "faith" (*tietis*) means, strictly speaking, "beliefs." For example, that Jesus marveled at the Roman centurion's "faith" means that he was surprised by the man's deep trust, not by the way he could rattle off a list of beliefs. He would have found it hard to do so. And when Jesus reproved the disciples for their "lack of faith," he meant their lack of trust and courage; it wasn't a reprimand for dropping one or another article of faith from the creed. The reason is obvious: No creed existed. No beliefs had been spelled out. Faith was courageous trust in Jesus and in the Good News which he lived and preached. Eventually this trust would crystallize into explicit beliefs, it is true. But the starting point is trusting courage, not beliefs. And in our life of faith just as in lighting a fuse, it makes a vital difference at which end we start.[6]

Closing the gap between beliefs and experience through the prayer of faith is not only of paramount importance, it is our first responsibility every day of our lives. The Word I preach must become incarnate in my own experience. It is the journey from Haran to Canaan, the pilgrimage from theory into reality, from unawareness to awareness, from idea into experience, from trivial concerns to unified consciousness with Jesus. As Christ is formed in us, we come to know him more deeply. "Maybe it sounds arrogant to say we come to know Christ as we persevere in contemplative prayer. But the truth is not less than this. We come to know what it is to live every moment, every decision, joy or difficulty from within his presence and so out of the infinite resources of this power—the power of love and compassion, an unshakeable reality."[7]

Many Christians never have grabbed aholt of God. They do not know—really know—that God dearly and passionately loves them. Many accept it theoretically; others in a shadowy sort of way. While their belief system is invulnerable, their faith in God's love for them is remote and abstract. They would be hard-pressed to say that the essence of their faith-commitment is a love affair between God and themselves. Not just a simple love affair but a *furious* love affair.

How do we grab aholt of God? How do we overcome our sadness and isolation? How do we develop the courage and generosity to treasure the signature of Jesus on the pages of our lives? How, how, how? The answer comes irresistibly and unmistakably: prayer.

"Seek first the kingdom of God" (see Matthew 6:33). This requires taking time out from family, friends, career, ministry, even "doing good" to enter into the great silence of God. Alone in that silence, the noise within will subside and the Voice of Love will be heard. Without such silence we will drown in the inner cacophony of dialogues, encounters, meetings, discussions, and conferences where there is much speaking and little listening.

Most of the Christians I meet, myself included, were raised in a devotional spirituality that encouraged external works of piety such as attending church, Bible reading, Scripture memorization, prayer groups, retreats, spiritual reading, and quiet times of confession, adoration, thanksgiving, and petition and intercession. These devotions aimed at developing and nurturing our relationship with God. They led to a biblical *metanoia*, the personal conversion we needed to undergo in order to become true disciples of Jesus. But, as Shannon notes, it was a metanoia of behavior—forsaking the self-indulgent lifestyle of fornication, sexual irresponsibility, feuds and wrangling, jealousy, greed, bad temper, quarrels, envy, drunkenness, orgies, and similar things,[8] and the sturdy effort to acquire the virtues and attitudes compatible with the mind of Christ. Devotional spirituality led to a new way of doing but not necessarily of seeing. It focused more on behavior than on consciousness; more on doing God's will and performing the devotional acts that pleased him than on experiencing God as God truly is. "A crude way of putting it would be to say that I spent so much time doing the things that would please God that I had no time left just to be with God."[9]

Acknowledging the critical importance of a spirituality of devotions and its many valuable insights, contemplative spirituality tends to emphasize the need for a change in consciousness, a new way of seeing God, others, self, and the world. It is not enough that we behave better; we must come to see reality differently.

For the majority of us, our prayer time is short and verbose. Too much talking and not enough listening—too much head and not enough heart. Contemplative prayer leads us in silence into the love that is at the center of our being. "We know from our human relationships how much faith we need to have in a person in order to be silent with them. We know that our faith in a person is deepened by such silence. This too is the dynamic of our silence in prayer—realizing God's love for us expressed in the love of Jesus, deepening our faith in his love."[10]

On the journey from belief to experience, it takes more effort to be still than to run. Most of us live such a frenetic lifestyle that we are afraid of stillness, silence, and solitude. Years ago, Anne Morrow Lindbergh wrote:

As far as the search for silence and solitude is concerned, we live in a negative atmosphere, as invisible, as all-pervasive and as enervating as high humidity in

an August afternoon. The world does not understand today, in either man or woman, the need to
be alone. How inexplicable it seems! Anything else
will be accepted as a better excuse. If one sets aside
time for a business appointment, a trip to the hair-
dresser, a social engagement, or a shopping expe-
dition, that time will be accepted as inviolable.
But if one says, "I cannot come because it is my
hour to be alone," one is considered rude, egotis-
tical, or strange. What a commentary on our civilization, when being alone is considered suspect;
when one has to apologize for it, make excuses,
hide the fact that one practices solitude—like a
secret vice.[11]

A certain existential panic can overtake us when we
first face the stillness, but if we can find the courage to
embrace it, we enter into the peace that is beyond all
understanding. On the other hand, if we cannot recognize
the value of simply being alone with God, as the beloved,
without doing anything, we gouge the heart out of
Christianity. Beliefs become more important than faith
and even small barriers create insurmountable obstacles
among Christians.

A simple method of contemplative prayer (often called
"centering prayer" in our time and anchored in the
Western Christian tradition of John Cassian and the
desert fathers and not, as some think, in Eastern mysticism
or New Age philosophy) has four steps:

1. Take a few minutes to relax your body and quiet your spirit. Then, in a simple act of faith, be present to God dwelling in the depths of your being.

2. Choose a single sacred word or phrase that captures something of the flavor of your intimate relationship with God. A word such as *Jesus, Abba, Peace, God,* or a phrase such as *Abba, I belong to you* or *Help me to live in your presence,* etc. Without moving your lips, repeat the sacred word inwardly, slowly, and often.

3. When distractions come, as they inevitably will (even in the most advanced prayers) simply return to listening to your sacred word. Picture yourself sitting quietly in a rowboat in the center of a placid lake. All is still and quiet. Suddenly a speedboat roars by about fifty yards on your starboard side. The ripple of its waves rocks your little rowboat violently. The ripple represents the wanderings of the mind. Again, gently return to your sacred word.

4. After a twenty-minute period of prayer, conclude with the Lord's Prayer, a favorite psalm, or some spontaneous words of praise and thanks.

Contemporary spiritual masters recommend two twenty-minute periods of contemplative prayer each day. The ideal times are the hour before breakfast and the hour before dinner. Because of the psychosomatic unity of body, mind, and spirit, a feeling of physical hunger is helpful. It awakens the soul's longing for God. As the psychiatrist Psichari once said, "The best preparation for prayer is a handful of dates and a glass of water," a metaphor for a relatively empty stomach.

And do not evaluate, measure, or judge your periods of contemplative prayer. In our achievement-oriented society, we'll probably begin to pray with a superficial concern for results in a futile attempt to discern if our investment of time and energy was worth it: Did it produce any luminous insight or any extraordinary experience? That kind of spiritual materialism will disappear, the ego will be purified, and self-consciousness will fade through the practice of daily prayer.

Just show up and shut up.

Whatever else it may be, prayer is first and foremost an act of love. Beyond any pragmatic considerations, prayer is personal response to the love of God. To love someone implies a longing for presence and communion. "Yet the news about him spread all the more, so that crowds of people came to hear him and to be healed of their sicknesses. But Jesus often withdrew to lonely places and prayed" (Luke 5:15–16). Jesus prayed primarily because he loved his Father. To be like Christ is to be a Christian.

No matter how overextended we are, we manage to make time for the people who matter to us. (In the past twenty years I have visited Chicago dozens of times and never have failed once to spend the night with my dear ninety-year-old friend, Frances Brennan.) As Woody Allen once said, "Eighty percent of life is showing up." Why? Because simply showing up is a kind of loving. The readiness to conscientiously waste time with a friend is a silent affirmation of their importance in our lives. Basil Pennington captures the simplicity of this gesture:

A father is delighted when his little one, leaving off his toys and friends, runs to him and climbs into his arms. As he holds his little one close to him, he cares little whether the child is looking around, his attention flitting from one thing to another, or just settling down to sleep. Essentially the child is choosing to be with his father, confident of the love, the care, the security, that is there in those arms. Contemplative prayer is much like that. We settle down in our Father's arms, in his loving hands. Our mind, our thoughts, our imagination may flit about here and there; we might even fall asleep; but essentially we are choosing to remain for this time intimately with our Father, giving ourselves to him, receiving his love and care, letting him enjoy us as he will. It is very simple prayer. It is very childlike prayer. It is prayer that opens us out to all the delights of the Kingdom.[12]

One of the four cardinal rules in prayer is the dictum of Dom Chapman: Pray as you can; don't pray as you can't. We must find our own way. Experimentation is indispensable if we are to find the method best suited to our needs and temperament. The mode and manner of prayer can differ radically, even with people who live in the same town and have the identical cultural background. C. S. Lewis was bewildered at Rose Macauley's prayer life. He admits he never could and never would want to pray like her. "Like you," he writes to Malcolm, "I was staggered by her continual search for more and more prayers. If she were merely collecting them as *objects d'art,* I could understand it; she was a born collector. But I get the impression that she collected them in order to use them; that her whole prayer life depended on what we may call ready-made prayers—prayers written by other people."[13]

On this issue I stand on the same side of the street as C. S. Lewis, while accepting that a great many other people besides Rose Macauley have been helped by ready-made prayers. An elderly nun once told the religious superior of her convent that all she was able to do during her prayer time was to repeat the Lord's Prayer over and over. But Teresa of Avila quickly discerned that she has scaled the heights of contemplative prayer. Once again, pray as you can; don't pray as you can't.

For people whose personality and temperament are more congenial with a structured method of prayer, let me propose another way that has proven effective (based on personal correspondence) with thousands of Christians. This approach to praying has four stages:

1. *Let yourself be loved by God.* Prayer begins with the appreciation and realization of the concrete meaning of God's love for me just as I am and not as I should be. His love is not based on my performance. I haven't earned it; therefore, I can't lose it. The first stage of prayer is not an activity of mind but a passive mode of receiving. Like slipping into a tub of hot water, I let God's love seep in, saturate, permeate every part of my being. It is one thing to know he loves me and quite another thing to experience it in faith. As I grow still, I will be grabbed aholt of by God: "I am your God, you are my child. How can you ever doubt that

I will embrace you again, hold you against my breast, kiss you, and let my hands run through your hair. I am a God of mercy and compassion, of tenderness and care. I so much want you to be close to me. I know all your thoughts. I hear all your words. I see all of your actions. And I love you. Do not judge yourself. Do not condemn yourself. Do not reject yourself. Let my love touch the most hidden corners of your heart and reveal to you your beauty, a beauty that you have lost sight of. Come, let me wipe away your tears, and let my mouth come close to your ear and say to you, 'I love, I love you, I love you.'"[14]

2. *Respond to God's love through adoration.* This is the highest and most intense activity that any human being is capable of. To adore is to abandon myself completely to the loving hands of God. When Henri Nouwen asked his spiritual guide, "How do I live a life in which Jesus is truly the center?" the reply came, "Be faithful in your adoration":

> This word makes it clear that all my attention must be on Jesus, not on myself. To adore is to be drawn away from my own preoccupations into the presence of Jesus. It means letting go of what I want, desire, or have planned, and fully trusting Jesus and his love.[15]

He can do with me what he wants. In the Lord's Prayer when I pray, "Thy will be done," I can pray these words without fear or apprehension because I am convinced that my Abba is no threat to me, that he is the course of my life and fulfillment. The prayer of adoration can be made with words or without words, in my own words or the words of another.

3. Meditate on a gospel passage. Meditation is thinking and reflecting about God. Prayer is speaking and listening to God. Read no more than five or ten verses of a gospel (this is not a time for Bible study). Identify with some person in the passage, and raise the question, *What is Jesus saying to me in this text?*

Illustration: I read Matthew 5:1–3. "Now when he saw the crowds, he went up on a mountainside and sat down. His disciples came to him, and he began to teach them saying: 'Blessed are the poor in spirit, for theirs is the kingdom of heaven.'" I identify myself as one of the disciples. Jesus looks me directly in the eye and tells me I am blessed if I am poor in spirit. These are Jesus' first words in his inaugural address. Obviously they are of immense importance to him, and so should they be for me. What does it mean, "being poor in spirit"? I get in touch with my past and begin to meditate.

I trip back down memory lane to Praise Gathering '91 at the Indianapolis Convention Center. After I delivered a forty-minute sermon entitled "The Victorious Limp," the assembled community of eleven thousand rose to its feet and erupted into thunderous applause. My shadow self that hungers for honor, recognition, power, glory, and human respect experienced an instant of gratification. My false self—which thrives on the illusion that my real identity lies in ministerial success, homiletic triumph, victories in the vineyard, stellar book reviews, and the admiration of others—basked in the chorus of adulation.

In that fleeting moment of euphoria, God took pity on his poor, proud son. Immediately I was given a vision of myself lying in a coffin. The funeral home had closed, the place was deserted. My embalmed body was lying in the coffin completely alone. I had run out of time.

The experience was neither macabre nor morbid; rather, it was a moment of supreme liberation from the false self. My imagined identity was unmasked in absurdity. We discover by force of death that there is no substance under the things with which we are clothed. I am hollow and my structure of pleasure and ambitions has no foundation. I am objectified in them. But they are all destined by their own contingency to be destroyed. "And when they are gone there will be nothing left of me but my own nakedness and emptiness and hollowness."[16]

Blessed are the poor in spirit. The poor man and woman are in touch with their naked poverty and transcendental neediness.

As I stared at my lifeless body I remembered a story about a bishop who lay dying in his bed—with all his episcopal vestments on! The applause of the eleven thousand continued and I started to laugh—at myself for wearing my miter to the Praise Gathering.

Peter Van Breemen writes, "The poor man accepts himself. He has a self-image in which the awareness of his limitations is very vivid, but that does not depress him. This consciousness of his own insufficiency without feelings of self-hatred is typical of the poor in spirit."[17]

4. *Close with a prayer of intercession/petition.* Interceding and pleading is not rattling off a grocery list of needy people and

worthy projects. Praying for others is shedding our blood, spending ourselves without counting the cost in empathy and compassion. It is also sinking into the mind of Jesus, uniting ourselves in his prayer of intercession. We experience the unutterable groans of the Spirit in our own hearts. "And the greater our empathy and the more closely we identify through compassion with those for whom we pray, the more perfect is our communion with the merciful God."[18]

Never let a day pass without praying for yourself for an increase of faith.

Conclude your prayer by returning to the second stage of adoration—thanking God for his goodness, praising him for his forgiveness, telling him you love him and will try to serve him one day at a time. Again, the recommended time frame for this kind of structured prayer is twenty minutes twice a day.

A simple mnemonic device may be helpful here. The five P's. Insofar as possible, choose the same *place* for daily prayer, the same *period* of time, the same *posture* (standing, sitting, kneeling, or—as with Ignatius of Loyola—lying on your back), select a *passage* from Scripture, and *pray*.

Let me close this chapter with the four cardinal rules of prayer:

1. The most important is, one learns to pray by praying. What is crucial is that we are really on the journey, not just thinking about the journey or reading or talking about it. "One faltering but actual step is more valuable than any number of journeys performed in the imagination."[19]

2. As mentioned earlier, pray as you can; don't pray as you can't.

3. Don't just pray when you feel like it. Showing up and shutting up is a discipline. Each day that rests on the twin pillars of the morning and evening prayer is a step on the journey from beliefs to experience, from theory to reality. As the Nike commercial said, "Just do it."

4. When a man or woman has an intense desire to grab aholt of God, they move and act. They respond and pray. Without that hunger, they are dilettantes playing spiritual games. If the intense desire is lacking, fall on your knees to the God you half-believe in and beg for the gift. As the late Rabbi Abraham Heschel remarked, "God is of no importance unless he is of supreme importance."

Contemplative prayer is an all-out onslaught on egoism, isolation, and melancholy. Forgetting about oneself seems so simple, yet it demands nothing less than the crucifixion of the ego. The renunciation of self-consciousness in order to acquire Christ-consciousness comes at great cost—losing your life to find your life (see Mark 8:35). But it brings the great assurance that the signature of Jesus is written even on the pages of our prayer lives.

Chapter Twelve

LAZARUS
LAUGHED!

ONE SUMMER in Iowa City, I directed a five-day retreat for a little band of Christians. The small number of participants allowed for an unusual degree of dialogue, sharing, and interpersonal communion. One mid-thirtyish woman in the group was conspicuous by her silence. She was a slender, attractive nun who neither smiled nor sighed, laughed nor cried, reacted, responded, nor communicated with any of us.

On the afternoon of the fourth day I invited each person to share what the Lord had been doing in his or her life the past few days. After a couple of minutes of silence, the uncommunicative nun, whom I shall call Christine, reached for her journal and said, "Something happened to me yesterday, and I wrote it down. You were speaking, Brennan, on the compassion of Jesus. You developed the two images of husband and lover found in Isaiah 54 and Hosea 2. Then you quoted the words of St. Augustine, 'Christ is the best husband.'

"At the end of your talk, you prayed that we might experience what you had just shared. You asked us to close our eyes. Almost the moment I did, something happened. In faith I was transported into a large ballroom filled with people. I was sitting by myself on a wooden chair, when a man approached me, took my hand, and led me onto the floor. He held me in his arms and led me in the dance.

"The tempo of the music increased, and we whirled faster and faster. The man's eyes never left my face. His radiant smile covered me with warmth, delight, and a sense of acceptance. Everyone else on the floor stopped dancing. They were staring at us. The beat of the music increased, and we pirouetted around the room in reckless rhythm. I glanced at his hands, and then I knew. Brilliant wounds of a battle long ago, almost like a signature carved in flesh. The music tapered to a slow, lilting melody, and Jesus rocked me back and forth. As the dance ended, he pulled me close to him. Do you know what he whispered?"

At this moment every retreatant in the chapel strained forward. Tears rolled down Christine's cheeks. A full minute of silence ensued. Though her face was beaming, the tears kept falling. Finally she spoke, "Jesus whispered to me, 'Christine, I'm wild about you.'"

She continued, "I stayed here in chapel for over an

hour, then went to my room and began to write in my journal what I had just experienced. Suddenly it seemed as if the pen were lifted from my fingers. Again in faith I heard Jesus say, 'I'm really wild about you.' It was a new experience once more. The love of Jesus swept over me like a gentle tide saturating my being in wonder, bewilderment, peace, certitude, and deep worship."

For Christine it was the release of the Holy Spirit elevating her faith and love to a new plateau. It was a decisive breakthrough into a personal relationship with Christ as her husband and lover. Ignatius of Loyola would describe it as a moment of "immense consolation." Spiritual writers today would speak of a "mountaintop" experience, an encounter with *mysterium tremendum*. Karl Rahner would simply call her a mystic—one who has experienced something.

What caught my attention in Christine's narrative was that the Jesus she encountered was smiling. Did Jesus smile? Did he actually laugh?

The Gospels never mention his doing either. They do testify that he wept twice—over Jerusalem and Lazarus, his city and his friend. Is it likely, however, that this sacred man, like us in all things but ungratefulness, could have wept from sorrow but not laughed for joy? Could Jesus have failed to smile when a child cuddled up in his arms? Or when the headwaiter at Cana nearly fainted at the six hundred gallons of vintage wine? Or when he saw Zacchaeus out on a limb? Or when Peter put his foot in his mouth one more time?

I simply cannot believe that Jesus did not laugh when

he saw something funny or smile when he experienced in his being the love of his Abba. He attracted not only a leading Pharisee and a Roman centurion but also children and simple folk like Mary Magdalene. Our human experience tells us that Jesus could not have done that if he always wore the solemn face of a mourner or the stern mask of a judge, if his face did not often crease into a smile and his whole body erupt in merry laughter.

Yet how many paintings are there in the history of Christian art that portray a smiling Savior? Where in our songbooks and prayer books are there odes to a laughing Christ? We readily recall him as "a man of sorrow" and forget how much joy his presence brought to sinners and party-goers, to the sick and the dying. Undoubtedly, Jesus laughed. He probably laughs at us when we rob discipleship of its playfulness and pull long faces like dignitaries at a state funeral.

Several years ago on a private retreat, I jotted down a short Easter meditation based on John 20:1–10. It reads:

> Early Sunday morning, as the sun begins to streak across the eastern sky, the stiff body—the chest begins to heave—a hand moves up slowly and uncovers his face—he adjusts to the darkness—stands up shakily—passes out of the tomb. Outside, he breathes the fresh air—he thrills to his new experience—he looks up to the hill and sees three empty crosses. He smiles and walks away. The risen Christ is the smiling Christ.

Teresa of Avila wrote, "When the Lord showed himself to me, his body was always risen and glorified." Is it surprising that the Lord of glory who whirled Christine around the dance floor is a radiantly happy and smiling Christ?

Nevertheless, an intense Christian might protest, "Why is it important to establish whether Jesus smiled or not? It seems to me this is much ado about nothing. Let us move on to more urgent evangelical concerns."

The question of Jesus' joyfulness is not trivial for this reason: Prayer is a personal response to loving presence. When the Jesus of our journey is the smiling Christ, when we respond to his whispered word, "I'm wild about you," the process of inner healing can begin. He heals us of our absorption in ourselves—where we take ourselves too seriously, where the days and nights revolve around us, our heartaches and hiatal hernias, our problems and frustrations. His smile allows us to distance ourselves from ourselves and see ourselves in perspective as we really are. We are creatures fearfully and wonderfully made, a bundle of paradoxes and contradictions.

The story of the raising of Lazarus (see John 11) begins with his two sisters, Martha and Mary, sending word to Jesus: "Lord, the man you love is ill."

When Jesus arrives in Bethany, Mary is told, "The Master is here and wants to see you."

She goes to Jesus and throws herself at his feet saying, "Lord, if You had been here, my brother would not have died."

At the sight of her tears, with a sigh that comes straight from his heart, Jesus asks, "Where is he?"

Mary says, "Lord, come and see."

Jesus weeps.

And the Jews say, "See how much he loved him."

In 1981, Roslyn and I made a silent eight-day directed retreat at the renewal center in Grand Coteau, Louisiana. Roslyn sent word to Jesus, "Lord, the man you love is ill."

When Jesus arrived in Grand Coteau, he learned that Brennan was in the depths of desolation. I was in an agony of indecision. Should Roslyn and I marry? I loved her with all my heart, but the demon of self-deception is subtle. Was it the Father's will for us to marry or my own will? How could I be certain I had heard God's voice? Besides, what does the canon law of the Catholic church say? And what will people say—parents, relatives, friends, the thousands who have heard me preach the gospel? I was torn up inside, shrouded in darkness and confusion.

Word was sent to Roslyn: "The teacher is here and asking for you." As soon as she heard this, she got up and started out in his direction. When she came to the place where Jesus was, she fell at his feet and said, "Lord, my Brennan's heart is broken with grief. He is troubled, confused, and despairing. If you had been here, he would not be like this." Roslyn started to cry.

When Jesus saw her weeping, he was troubled in spirit, moved by the deepest emotions. "Where is he?" Jesus asked.

"He is in the chapel. Come, I'll show you where it is."

Jesus himself began to cry. In the distance, some others

on retreat whispered, "See how much he loves them."

Jesus approached the chapel and opened the door. "Let us be alone," he said to Roslyn. I was so caught up in my inner turmoil that I didn't notice him as he came and sat down beside me.

He took my hand. Startled, I turned and looked at him. He did not say a word. He placed his other hand on top of mine. Then he smiled. Oh, how I wish you could have been there! The delight on his face and the merriment in his eyes dispelled every trace of doubt and confusion. In an instant I went from darkest night to sunny noonday. Though he did not speak, his smile spoke: "Do not be afraid. I am with you." I walked out of the chapel feeling like Lazarus emerging from the tomb.

The smiling Christ heals and liberates. With newly discovered delight in ourselves, we go out to our brothers and sisters as we are, where they are, and minister the smiling Christ to them. Not far away from us, there is someone who is afraid and needs our courage, someone who is lonely and needs our presence. There is someone hurt, needing our healing; unloved, needing our touching; old, needing to feel that we care; weak, needing the support of our shared weakness. One of the most healing words I ever spoke as a confessor was to an old priest with a drinking problem.

"Just a few years ago," I said, "I was a hopeless alcoholic in the gutter in Fort Lauderdale."

"You?" he cried. "O thank God!"

When we bring a smile to the face of someone in pain, we have brought Christ to them.

Eugene O'Neill once wrote a muddled play with a

splendid ending. It dealt with the life of Lazarus after Jesus summoned him from the grave. O'Neill called his play *Lazarus Laughed*. It is the story of a lover of Jesus who had tasted death and seen it for what it is. "Laugh with me! Death is dead! Fear is no more! There is only life! There is only laughter!" And, O'Neill tells us, Lazarus begins to laugh—softly at first, then full-throated: "A laugh so full of complete acceptance of life, a profound assertion of joy in living, so devoid of all fear, that it is infectious with love, so infectious that, despite themselves, his listeners are caught up by it and carried away."[1]

Laughter is not hysteria. Laughter is not a belly explosion over a vulgar joke. Laughter is...joy in living. Paschal spirituality says to the Christian, *You can laugh, you can take delight in living.* Why? "Because in the midst of death you are constantly discovering life: in a glance or a touch or a song, in a field of corn or a friend who cares, in the moon or an amoeba, in a lifeless loaf suddenly become the body of Christ."[2]

Christianity calls for risen Christians, disciples like the hero of Eugene O'Neill's play. Lazarus has tasted death and seen it for what it is. Now his joy in living is irresistible.

> Laugh with me!
> Death is dead!
> Fear is no more!
> There is only life!
> There is only laughter!

If darkest night is upon you as you read these words, know that the risen Jesus is wild about you, even if you can't feel it. Listen beneath your pain for the voice of Abba God: "Make ready for my Christ whose smile, like lightning, sets free the song of everlasting glory that now sleeps in your paper flesh like dynamite."

A CLOSING WORD

On THE LAST NIGHT of a silent eight-day retreat in the snowy landscape of eastern Pennsylvania, I had a dream so vivid that it awakened me from a sound sleep. I went to my desk to capture on paper the words and images from the dream. Here's what I had written:

> In my mind's eye, I see a man entering the gas chamber in San Quentin, a woman being seated in the electric chair at an unidentified prison. I see the ovens at Auschwitz and Dachau and trucks piled high with bodies. I see Hiroshima and ninety-five thousand burnt bodies, charred beyond recognition,

littering the streets and hillsides. I see the crumpled body of John F. Kennedy. I see the coffin of John Wayne surrounded by Hollywood glitterati. Now I see rows of crosses outside the city wall of old Jerusalem with hundreds of bodies nailed to them— thieves, seditionists, murderers. On a hill I see three more crosses with the bodies of three more men and they look the same, though the man in the middle seems to have been brutalized a bit more than the others.

Two days later. I'm in the main square of a large city. A group of men are running around, shouting the most preposterous thing—the crucifixion of the man in the middle of the three crosses was not just another political execution. They are saying it is the most important event in history. They are saying that the man is now the focal point of faith and the object of worship for men and women for all time to come.

I am bewildered. I return to that hillside. As I stand there staring up at what is now an empty cross, away in the distance a man steps over the rim of the horizon. From somewhere a mighty chorus is singing, "King of kings and Lord of lords."

I look around. I am no longer alone. As far as the eye can see, the landscape is dotted with people. And they are all singing, "King of kings and Lord of lords." The Man comes striding into focus. He is bathed in light. As if two curtains were being drawn aside, the skies open and are filled with the most beautiful beings I have ever seen. They begin a rhythmic chant: "Lord Jesus Christ, God-hero, Lord Jesus Christ, God-hero, God-hero..."

The roar swells and fills every echo chamber of the universe. I look at the Man. His face is aglow like a sunburst over the Sandias, his eyes are like two north stars.

"Peace be to you," he says. His words are more of a command than a greeting. "I know all about each one of you. I knew you when you were awake and asleep, when you were at home and on vacation. Before a word was on the tip of your tongue I knew the whole of it. I watched your every movement. With all your ways I am familiar."

The roll call begins...

I see Sandi Patti step forward, followed by Madonna. I see Saddam Hussein and Mother Teresa. Next come Adolf Hitler and Mohandas Gandhi. Idi Amin and Billy Graham. Following them is Martin Luther and Frank Sinatra (he's not singing, "We'll do it my way"), the prophet Amos and Hugh Hefner, Jeremiah and Johnny Carson, Mary and Joseph, George and Barbara Bush, Peter, James, John and Stalin, Churchill and Roosevelt.

On and on it goes. All the famous, powerful people who have ever lived and the millions of unsung, uncelebrated ones...everyone who has ever lived. I hear my name: "Brennan." As I step forward, like a bell sounding deep in my soul, I hear the words of the poet T. S. Eliot, "O my soul, be prepared to meet him who knows how to ask questions."

The Man looks directly at me and then looks through all my bluff and pious rhetoric, through the content of my books and sermons, through all the minimizing and justifying of my lifestyle. For the first time in my life, I am seen and known as I really am.

Trembling, I ask, "What is my judgment, Lord?"

He hands me the Book. "The word I spoke has already judged you." A long pause...then he smiles. I walk up to him and touch his face. He takes my hand and we go home.

I smile, Lord Jesus, as I put these words on paper on this icy wintry night in Wernersville, Pennsylvania. Glory and praise to you.

The content of this dream is more real than the book you are holding in your hand. On a given day at a specific hour known only to the Father (see Matthew 24:36), Jesus Christ will return in glory. *Every man and woman who has ever drawn breath will be appraised, evaluated, and measured solely in terms of their relationship with the Carpenter from Nazareth.* This is the realm of the really Real. This dream is neither the product of a vivid imagination nor a comatose religious fantasy conjured up to satisfy an emotional need. The eschatological lordship of Jesus Christ and his primacy in the created order (see Ephesians 1:9–10) are at the very heart of the gospel proclamation. This is reality.

If I ask myself, "What am I doing walking around this planet? Why do I exist?" as a disciple of Jesus I must answer, "For the sake of Christ." If the angels ask, it is the same answer: "We exist for the sake of Jesus Christ." If the entire universe were suddenly to become articulate, from north to south and east to west, it would cry out in chorus, "We exist for the sake of Christ!" The name of Jesus would issue from the seas and mountains and valleys; it would be tapped out by the pattering rain. It would be written in the skies by the lightning. The storms would roar the name "Jesus Christ, God-hero!" and the mountains would echo it back. The sun on its westward march through the heavens would chant a thunderous hymn: "The whole universe is full of Christ!"

This is the apostle Paul's vision of creation, his Christocentric concept of the universe: "He is the image of the invisible God, the firstborn over all creation. For by him all things were created: things in heaven and on earth, visible and invisible, whether thrones or powers or rulers or authorities; *all things were created by him and for him*" (Colossians 1:15–16, italics mine).

If there is any priority in the personal or professional life of a Christian more important than the lordship of Jesus Christ, he or she is disqualified as a witness to the gospel. Since that glorious morning when Jesus burst the bonds of death and the messianic era erupted into history, there has been a new agenda, new priorities, and a revolutionary hierarchy of values.

The Nazarene Carpenter did not simply refine Aristotelian ethics; he did not merely reorder Old

Testament spirituality; he did not simply renovate the old creation. He initiated a revolution. We must renounce all that we possess, not just most of it (see Luke 14:33). We must give up the old way of life, not just correct some aberrations in it (see Ephesians 4:22). We are to be an altogether new creation, not simply a refurbished version of it (see Galatians 6:15). We are to be transformed from one glory to another, even into the very image of the Lord-transparent (see 2 Corinthians 3:18). Our minds are to be renewed by a spiritual revolution (see Ephesians 4:23).

The primal sin, of course, is to go on acting like it never happened, basing our lives on pop religion and the power of positive thinking, trendy spiritualities and power politics, rather than on the Sermon on the Mount and the death and resurrection of Jesus Christ.

As a radical alternative this book is offered to Christians who want to live by faith and not by mere "religion," for those who recognize that many of the burning theological issues in the church today are neither burning nor theological; who see Christianity neither as a moral code or a belief system but as a love affair; who have not forgotten that they are followers of a crucified Christ; who know that following him means living dangerously; who want to live the gospel without compromise; who have no greater desire than to have his signature written on the pages of their lives.

NOTES

AN OPENING WORD

1. Ernst Kasemann, *Jesus Means Freedom* (Philadelphia: Fortress Press, 1969), 77.

2. Walter J. Burghardt, *Still Proclaiming Your Wonders* (Ramsey, NJ: Paulist Press, 1984), 136.

3. William Barry, *Finding God in All Things* (Notre Dame, IN: Ave Maria Press, 1991), 97–98.

4. Thomas Merton, *Seeds of Contemplation* (New York: Panthea Books, 1956), 62.

5. Alan Jones, *Exploring Spiritual Direction* (New York: Winston-Seabury Press, 1982), 73–74.

6. J. D. Salinger, *Franny and Zooey* (New York: Bantam Books, 1964), 109. Cited in Barry, *Finding God in All Things,* 98.

CHAPTER ONE: FROM HARAN TO CANAAN

1. Peter Van Breemen, *Called by Name* (Denville, NJ: Dimension Books, 1976), 8.

2. Daniel Taylor, *The Myth of Certainty* (Waco, TX: Jarrell, 1986), 134.

3. Eugene Kennedy, *The Choice to Be Human: Jesus Alive in Matthew's Gospel* (New York: Doubleday, 1988), 211–212.

4. Van Breemen, *Called by Name,* 16.

5. Louis Evely, *That Man Is You* (Ramsey/Toronto: Paulist Press, 1967), 114.

6. James Mackey, *Jesus: The Man and the Myth* (New York/Ramsey: Paulist Press, 1979), 274–275. Here I have relied heavily on the careful scholarship of Mackey for the treatment of the genealogy of Jesus.

7. Stephen Arterburn and Jack Felton, *Toxic Faith: Understanding and Overcoming Religious Addiction* (Nashville, TN: Oliver Nelson Books, 1991), 72–73.

8. Mackey, *Jesus: The Man and the Myth,* 278.

9. Walter Brueggemann, *The Prophetic Imagination* (Philadelphia: Fortress Press, 1978), 112.

10. Albert Nolan, *Jesus Before Christianity* (Maryknoll, NY: Orbis Books, 1978), 136.

11. Ibid., 137.

12. Kennedy, *The Choice to Be Human,* 213–214.

13. Brennan Manning, *Lion and Lamb: The Relentless Tenderness of Jesus* (Old Tappan, NJ: Revell, 1986), 33–34.

CHAPTER TWO: THE SIGNATURE OF JESUS

1. Francis Thompson, "The Hound of Heaven," *Representative Poetry Online.* http://eir.library.utoronto.ca/rpo/display/poem2204.html (accessed December 8, 2003).

2. Dietrich Bonhoeffer, *The Cost of Discipleship* (New York: Simon & Schuster, 1995). First published in German in 1937.

3. William Penn, quoted in *The Doubleday Christian Quotation Collection* (New York: Doubleday, 1998), 151.

4. Bonhoeffer, *The Cost of Discipleship.*

5. Kasemann, *Jesus Means Freedom,* 176.

6. Dietrich Bonhoeffer, *Letters and Papers from Prison* (London: SCM Press, 1971), 279.

7. John Shea, *The Challenge of Jesus* (Chicago: Thomas More Press, 1984), 178.

8. Jim Wallis, *The Call to Conversion* (New York: Harper and Row, 1981), 43.

9. *Man of La Mancha* (1965), book by Dale Wasserman, music by Mitch Leigh, lyrics by Joe Darion.

CHAPTER THREE: POWER AND WISDOM

1. Flannery O'Connor, "A Good Man Is Hard to Find," in *Flannery O'Connor: The Complete Stories* (New York: Farrar, Strauss, and Giroux, 1972), 131.

2. *The Sermons of John Chrysostom,* quoted by George Montague in *The Living Thought of St. Paul* (Englewood, NJ: Prentice Hall, 1962), 78.

3. Jürgen Moltmann, *The Crucified God,* translated by R. A. Wilson and John Bowden from the German (New York: Harper and Row, 1974), 154.

4. John L. McKenzie, *The Power and the Wisdom* (Milwaukee: Bruce Publishing, 1965), 188.

5. Henri Nouwen, *Here and Now* (New York: Crossroad, 1995), 62.

6. Francis de Sales, *Living the Devout Life* (New York: Sheed and Ward, 1948), 115.

CHAPTER FOUR: FOOLS FOR CHRIST

1. Walter Wink, *Unmasking the Powers: The Invisible Forces That Determine Human Existence* (Philadelphia: Fortress Press, 1986), 105.

2. John Kavanaugh, S. J., gave a splendid address on radical Christianity at Fordham University in August 1985. In this chapter I have quoted from his paper and applied his ideas to the theme of the chapter.

3. Thomas Merton, *The Hidden Ground of Love* (New York: Farrar, Straus, and Giroux, 1985), 112.

4. John L. McKenzie, *The Civilization of Christianity* (Chicago: Thomas More Press, 1986), 66.

5. "Profiles and Personalities," *People*, March 9, 1987.
6. McKenzie, *The Civilization of Christianity*, 56.
7. Ibid., 242.
8. Kavanaugh, address on radical Christianity, 9.
9. Mark Twain, "The War Prayer," quoted in McKenzie, *The Civilization of Christianity*, 127.
10. Merton, *The Hidden Ground of Love*, 211.
11. Kavanaugh, address on radical Christianity, 12.
12. Parker J. Palmer, *The Promise of Paradox: A Celebration of Contradictions in the Christian Life* (Notre Dame, IN: Ave Maria Press, 1980), 81.
13. M. Scott Peck, *The Different Drum* (New York: Simon and Schuster, 1987), 233.
14. Wallis, *The Call to Conversion,* 178.

CHAPTER FIVE: DISCIPLESHIP TODAY

1. Thomas N. Hart, *To Know and Follow Jesus* (Mahwah, NJ: Paulist Press, 1985), 33.
2. Thomas R. Kelly, *A Testament of Devotion* (New York: Harper and Row, 1941), 58.
3. Ibid., 53–54.
4. Donald Gray, *Jesus, the Way to Freedom* (Winona, MN: St. Mary's Press, 1979), 38.
5. Keith Miller, *The Scent of Love* (Waco, TX: Word Books, 1983), quoted in Peck, *The Different Drum*, 294.
6. Strob Talbot, "Ethics in the Corporate World," *Time*, May 25, 1987.
7. Kelly, *A Testament of Devotion*, 114.

CHAPTER SIX: PASCHAL SPIRITUALITY

1. William J. Bausch, *Storytelling, Imagination, and Faith* (Mystic, CT: Twenty-Third Publications, 1984), 141.
2. John Heagle, *On the Way* (Chicago: Thomas More Press, 1981), 34.
3. Raymond E. Brown, *The Churches the Apostles Left Behind* (Mahwah, NJ: Paulist Press, 1984), 91.

4. Bausch, *Storytelling, Imagination, and Faith*, 29.
5. Kennedy, *The Choice to Be Human*, 130.
6. "My Favorite Things" from *The Sound of Music* (1959), music by Richard Rodgers, lyrics by Oscar Hammerstein II.
7. Peck, *The Different Drum*, 295.
8. Martin Marty, *Context: A Commentary on the Interaction of Religion and Culture* (Chicago: Claretian Publications, 1987), 5.
9. See Peter Van Breemen, *Certain as the Dawn* (Denville, NJ: Dimension Books, 1980).
10. Heagle, *On the Way*, 210.

CHAPTER SEVEN: CELEBRATE THE DARKNESS
1. Anthony DeMello, S. J., *The Song of the Bird* (Anand, India: Gujarat Sahitya Prakash, distributed by Loyola University Press, Chicago, 1983), 130.
2. Merton, *Hidden Ground of Love*. Letter to Daniel Berrigen, March 10, 1968.
3. Anthony Bloom and Georges LeFevre, *The Courage to Pray* (Mahwah, NJ: Paulist Press, 1973), 17.
4. DeMello, *The Song of the Bird*, 134.
5. Alan Jones, *Soul Making: The Desert Way of Spirituality* (New York: Harper and Row, 1985), 177.
6. Ibid., 178.
7. Merton, *Hidden Ground of Love*. This quote is from a letter to Dom Francois Decroix, April 21, 1967.
8. Hans Küng, *On Being a Christian* (New York: Doubleday, 1976), 341–342.

CHAPTER EIGHT: THE LOVE OF JESUS
1. Burghardt, *Still Proclaiming Your Wonders*, 140.
2. Van Breemen, *Called by Name*, 43.
3. Peter Van Breemen, *As Bread That Is Broken* (Denville, NJ: Dimension Books, 1974), 28.
4. William Shakespeare, *As You Like It*, act II, scene 1.

CHAPTER NINE: THE DISCIPLINE OF THE SECRET

1. Walter J. Burghardt, *Grace on Crutches* (Mahwah, NJ: Paulist Press, 1986), 104. David H. C. Read says, "In my opinion, no one today can equal Walter Burghardt in expounding the gospel…with clarity, wit and craftily concealed scholarship." I would agree with that assessment.
2. Jaroslav Pelikan, *Jesus Through the Centuries* (New Haven, CT: Yale University Press, 1985), 155.
3. Peck, *The Different Drum,* 298.
4. For a full development of the discipline of the secret, see Geoffrey B. Kelly, *Liberating Faith* (Minneapolis, MN: Augsburg, 1984), 133ff.
5. Larry Rasmussen, "Worship in a World Come-of-Age," in *A Bonhoeffer Legacy: Essays in Understanding*, ed. A. J. Klassen (Grand Rapids, MI: William B. Eerdmans, 1981), 278.

CHAPTER TEN: THE COURAGE TO RISK

1. Alan Jones, *Exploring Spiritual Direction* (New York: Winston-Seabury Press, 1982), 115.
2. Tim Hansel, *You Gotta Keep Dancin'* (Elgin, IL: David C. Cook, 1985), 48.
3. The insight into this parable came from Christian psychologist and friend Molly Clark of Bastrop, Louisiana.
4. Myles Connolly, *Mr. Blue* (New York: Macmillan, 1928), 91.
5. Jones, *Exploring Spiritual Direction,* 39.

CHAPTER ELEVEN: GRABBING AHOLT OF GOD

1. William Reiser, *Into the Needle's Eye* (Notre Dame, IN: Ave Maria Press, 1984), 86.
2. Brother David Steindl-Rast, *Gratefulness: The Heart of Prayer* (Mahwah, NJ: Paulist Press, 1984), 64.
3. William H. Shannon, *Silence on Fire* (Crossroad, NY: Crossroad Publishing, 1991), 22.
4. Ibid., 23.
5. Walker Percy, self-interview, *Esquire,* June 1977.
6. Steindl-Rast, *Gratefulness: The Heart of Prayer,* 88–89.

7. Main, 115.
8. Galatians 5:19–20.
9. Shannon, *Silence on Fire*, 16.
10. Main, 45.
11. Anne Morrow Lindbergh, *Gift from the Sea* (New York: Random House, 1940), 24.
12. M. Basil Pennington, *Centering Prayer* (New York: Doubleday, 1980), 68–69.
13. C. S. Lewis, *Letters to Malcolm* (New York: Random House, 1966), 42.
14. An abbreviated version of Henri Nouwen, *The Primacy of the Heart* (Madison, WI: St. Benedict Center, 1988), 36–37.
15. Ibid., 20.
16. Thomas Merton, *New Seeds of Contemplation* (New York: New Directions, 1961), 35.
17. Van Breemen, 108.
18. Anthony Bloom, *The Courage to Pray* (New York: Paulist Press, 1973), 45.
19. Main, 77–78.

CHAPTER TWELVE: LAZARUS LAUGHED!
1. Eugene O'Neill, *Lazarus Laughed* (1928).
2. Burghardt, *Still Proclaiming Your Wonders*, 168.

Believing God's Unconditional Love

Most of us believe in God's grace—in theory. But somehow we can't seem to apply it in our daily lives. We continue to see Him as a small-minded bookkeeper, tallying our failures and successes on a score sheet. In *The Ragamuffin Gospel* Brennan Manning reminds us that nothing could be further from the truth. The Father beckons us to Himself with a "furious love" that burns brightly and constantly. Only when we truly embrace God's grace can we bask in the joy of a gospel that enfolds the most needy of His flock—the "ragamuffins."

ISBN: 1-59052-502-7